Praise for
The Heart Healer

"Hope and healing are of central importance to us as human beings. Without hope, life loses its luster and we are inclined to despair and give up. Healing is necessary for us to be restored and move forward. For anyone interested in helping others—or themselves for that matter—this book should be on your must-have list.

Cyndy Bartelli has taken one of the most complex subjects and given us a clear and pure understanding of how healing is possible in the midst of great pain. Not content to simply talk about a subject, she has provided solutions and action steps that can bring permanent healing.

It is not often that I can say, 'This book is for everyone.' In this case, I can. Everyone who has a friend who is experiencing heartache and every counselor or pastor who knows what it's like to try to bring hope again to those who have lost it needs this book. It is extremely well written, insightful, and practical. You will be thoroughly blessed when you read it—and who knows—you might get healed as well."

Pastor Chris Hayward
President
Cleansing Stream International

"Over the years, I have seen many Christ followers fall short of reaching their potential in life because they struggle with pain and hurt from their past. *The Heart Healer* is an anointed resource that combines the Word of God with the Spirit of God to help us overcome. The steps in "The Prayer" (chapter six) are simple but absolutely powerful. I've seen, firsthand, how God uses Cyndy and these "Heart Healing" principles to lead people in reaching their potential in life."

Pastor Randy Garcia
Fortress Church
San Antonio, TX

"Cyndy Bartelli has captured a simple yet profound truth of heart healing in her book *The Heart Healer*. Her stories are so real you will find yourself drawn into them. But these are not just stories used to illustrate a point; they are life-changing examples of how these principles actually can and do work for those that apply them. The need for heart healing is so great, yet Cyndy has been able to share in *The Heart Healer* the simple, attainable, and very practical steps to actually receive true heart healing. I highly recommend this book to everyone. Even if you don't think you need heart healing, you will receive good things from the Lord."

Pastor Doug Easterday
Father Heart of God Ministries

"Here is a book I have no hesitation in endorsing. When I first read the manuscript, I saw the potential for comfort and healing. Cyndy is a veteran in ministering to and helping hurting people. She is knowledgeable and qualified to write a book like this."

Ray Beeson
Director, Overcomers Ministries
and Author of *Strategic Spiritual Warfare*, *The Hidden Price of Greatness*, *The Real Battle*, and *Create in Me a Clean Heart*

"Being incredibly analytical and skeptical as I am, hearing that a prayer could heal heartache seemed very foreign to me. I came across this information and couldn't help but reflect on years of prolonged pain I'd experienced, and wonder if maybe this would help. This extremely simple book literally changed my life and how I handle past and current stress. I've been a Christian my whole life and never realized Jesus was in the heart-healing business this side of Heaven."

Rachael Hopkins, Los Angeles, CA

"This book is such a blessing! It is filled with many actual case histories and success stories and is divinely inspired. Written in concise and easy to understand guidelines, it is a book I strongly recommend to all, as we all carry scars from life. I cannot wait to share it with friends and family, and to re-read it myself."

KS Gac, Washington

"When I was asked to preview this book, I was delighted. And I was even more delighted after reading it. I've worked in inner healing and freedom ministry for 16 years, which changed my life forever. This book has given me a new tool in my tool belt, not only for myself, but to share with others. Everyone has memories that need healing. Cyndy's book shows us how to take those to The Heart Healer. I am going to need a case of these books for all the people I already plan to share them with."

Debi Lee, Texas

"Wow. Even after reading just a few chapters of the book, I began to realize ways I've thought about myself that held me back most of my life. When my wife and I prayed together for heart healing, God began to change me in big ways. What an experience! I feel different, like I'm free, with nothing holding me back from new ideas and new things God has for me."

Fernando Cortes, Texas

"It has been a blessing praying for Cyndy as the Lord gave her the words and examples to share with each one who reads this book. I have known her for many years and can say that the words she writes are straight from a very genuine place in her own heart. I, too, have been blessed to be a recipient of this healing and the freedom these prayers bring. It's easy to see that God is going to touch the lives of many people as they read *The Heart Healer*."

Mildred Whitmire, Texas

THE HEART HEALER

*God's Response to Personal Prayer
in a Hurting World*

CYNDY BARTELLI

Edited by Rachael Hopkins, Dr. Rayna Kneuper-Hall, and Jennifer Harshman
Book Design by James Woosley, FreeAgentPress.com

Disclaimer:
The author is not a medical doctor, psychiatrist, psychologist, pastor, nutritionist, or other mental or physical health care professional. The information provided in this book, or related videos, speaking engagements, and websites reflects the author's personal experiences, observations, and ongoing research.

Material in this book and all related messages is not a substitute for qualified professional care. Readers should continue all treatment received until released by those responsible for their well-being. Neither the author or the author's ministry take responsibility for any actions or non-actions of the readers based on the content of the book.

Any web addresses or links referenced in this book may have changed since publication.

The stories included in *The Heart Healer* are true. Names and other non-essential details were changed to protect the privacy of the contributors.

Published by Insignis Interactive
InsignisInteractive.com
Satsuma, Alabama 36572
VID: 20170715

This book is dedicated to:

My husband, Terry, who let me interrupt Texas Tech, San Antonio Spurs, and Dallas Cowboys games to discuss my work. This man was my greatest supporter.

Mildred, Virginia, Fernando, Rachael, Ray, and Doug, who selflessly provided prayer, encouragement, and critiques.

Loving friends and family members who encouraged me along the way.

Those who contributed their personal stories of heartbreak and healing. Without you, there wouldn't be a book to write.

ABOUT THE COVER

The jasper heart displayed on the cover was intentionally selected because it was prepared using the Kintsugi method. Kintsugi is an ancient Japanese art form using fine metal—in this case, gold—to restore a broken item to a beautiful, cherished piece. What once was broken is considered better than new because of its story and its history.

Additionally, the jasper stone referred to in the Old Testament of the Bible was considered symbolic of the glory of God.

The various layers and imperfections of the heart used on the cover represent a typical life journey and the gold repair lines in the shape of the cross remind us of the true Heart Healer.

Cover design by James Woosley
Cover photo by Adam Sayovitz and Danniebelle Cagas

CONTENTS

INTRODUCTION

THIS BOOK, ABOUT HOPE AND HEALING, began with a song. Although the church was filled with people, at that moment the song seemed for me alone as the words stirred a longing within, their meaning touching my soul. I suddenly knew. Change was coming. It would start with me.

Settling my hand over my heart, I repeated the words as a prayer—a prayer which began a journey taking me thousands of miles away to a place of increased understanding of God's healing power for the brokenhearted. Based on the words from "Hosanna" by Hillsong United, I formed my prayer.

> *Heal my heart, Lord, and cleanse me from things in my past that are not right in Your eyes. Open my own eyes to the future you have for me. Cause me to be sensitive to things that are important to You. Show me how to love others the same way You have shown your love to me. I set my destiny before You. Please be my Guide for eternity.*

If you are interested in making peace with your past and aligning your future toward good, I invite you to read the following pages with stories of others who prayed a simple prayer for healing. God heard them. He will hear you, too, and He will answer—perhaps in unexpected ways.

CHAPTER 1

BRAVE AND STRONG

AN AMBULANCE WAS COMING. My father sent me and my siblings to our bedrooms before it arrived. I hadn't seen our mom all day, but with my ear pressed against the door, I could hear her muffled voice mixed with his from their bedroom. The unmistakably deep voice of our family doctor joined theirs.

Sounds escalated as ambulance attendants entered the house. It soon became terrifyingly apparent our mother was being taken away.

As I heard the gurney roll by, our mother's whispered cries brought a flood of panic and fear into my fourteen-year-old heart. I began to sob. Trembling, I wondered: "What is going on? Where are they taking her?" The sound of the ambulance grew faint. I crumbled to the floor, staring across the room that once seemed bright.

Later, we learned of Mom's secret struggle with heartache so severe it culminated in a nervous breakdown. She was sent that day to a psychiatric hospital in a distant town, and we were unable to communicate with her in any way.

A busy schedule and pretty dresses masked my constant stress and did nothing to slow the tears falling on my pillow each night. As the eldest daughter, I struggled with new responsibilities I didn't know how to handle. Though five of us still lived in the house, it felt empty, and darkness hovered there for several months until Mom returned home.

Cuts and Bruises

Our parents' modest 1950s home bordered our subdivision in San Antonio, Texas. The back yard stretched along the eastern edge of an expanse of woods in gullies and canyons that sloped away from our subdivision as far as our young eyes could see. Dubbed "The Woods," it was our favorite place to play, and we would scramble down various pathways we had formed from frequent use. Scrub brush, oak trees, and mesquites filled The Woods. So did critters.

On summer nights, we would hear packs of wild dogs traveling through the dark woods in search of food. Parents would share tales of wild-dog sightings over our mutual chain-link fences as we stared with our neighbors into the darkness. It was said the wild dogs didn't venture out during the day, so if the sun was shining, my big brother, Buzzy (aka Carl), and I were usually found there.

Our mom laid out specific boundaries to keep us safe from the dreaded wild dogs in our personal playground. Occasionally, we rebelled against our mother's guidelines, risking wild-dog encounters for new adventures. Whether we played within those boundaries or rebelled in the wild-dog zone, "owies" were inevitable; returning home with cuts and bruises, we'd rush in looking for Mom.

We went to someone who loved us—one who we knew would make the pain all better.

As time passed, I accumulated the kinds of cuts and bruises no one else could see. Whether I lived life within safe boundaries or I rebelled in my personal "wild-dog zones," wounds from trials pierced my heart and left marks impacting my life for years. Although unseen, these wounds did far more damage than those requiring antiseptic and a bandage.

***

When I was a teenager, no one knew of my inner struggles. Although outwardly I looked like a happy high-school cheerleader, inwardly my world crumbled as I endured tremendous heartache at home. One year after the previous episode, Mom suffered a second nervous breakdown and was hospitalized again. I sensed life would never return to the way it was before.

Without hope, I often imagined letting go of the steering wheel while driving the family car; but, as I increased my speed, fear always stopped me—fear that I wouldn't actually die.

A couple of years after Mom's return, I was Homecoming Queen on the outside, but on the inside lived in daily fear of another episode of her illness. Smiles and efforts to achieve disguised the agony of worry and those secret thoughts of suicide.

***

Many decades and much additional heartache later, I've realized no one is exempt from distressing experiences. Whatever the source, as part of the human existence, we all deal with trauma, resulting in heartache and heartbreak.

And, we all wish we could go to someone who loves us—one who we know can make the pain all better.

Death, divorce, disease, disaster—trauma wounds our hearts, enormously affecting our souls and spirits.

Deep pain and heartache fueled my passion as I learned about life-changing prayer. Through each of my own heartfelt prayers, and prayers for many others, God gently unraveled a mystery for me: The need for *heart* healing and the resulting peace only He can provide.

The results were phenomenal. In just a few moments,

the abused, abandoned, and hopeless appealed to God with a simple prayer for heart healing. Peace settled over their past and their souls calmed. The core of the process involved recognizing the profound impact of our past hurts on our hearts. Our hearts matter!

The heart I'm referring to is not our physical heart. The word "heart" in the Bible is a figure of speech about our inner man—the whole person. Our biblical heart includes our mind, our will, and our emotions. As the center of our human spirit, our heart is the source of our thoughts and motivations, our emotions and courage and our resulting actions.

Through each of my own heartfelt prayers, and prayers for many others, God gently unraveled a mystery for me: The need for heart healing and the resulting peace only He can provide.

It is within this heart that we feel happy or sad, thrilled or frightened, fulfilled or broken. While the health of our physical heart is critical to our existence, the well-being of our emotional and spiritual heart is just as vital. It affects our mind, our will, and our emotions.

In the Bible, the heart is a matter of extreme importance to God. It is the most common term referencing humans. Here are just a few of the several hundred verses regarding it:

- "But if from there you seek the Lord your God, you will find him if you seek him with all your heart and with all your soul" (Deuteronomy 4:29 NIV).

- Samuel (an Old Testament prophet) wrote, "The Lord does not look at the things people look at. People look at the outward appearance, but the Lord looks at the heart" (1 Samuel 16:7 NIV).

- King Solomon said, "Above all else, guard your heart, for everything you do flows from it" (Proverbs 4:23 NIV).

- Jesus spoke these words, "For the mouth speaks what the heart is full of" (Matthew 12:34 NIV).

- "I am leaving you with a gift—peace of mind and heart. And the peace I give is a gift the world cannot give. So don't be troubled or afraid" (John 14:27 NLT).

Hearts live at the core of our beings, and God instructs us to treasure, protect, guard, and nurture them.

How do we treasure, protect, guard and nurture them? We may carefully select what we expose ourselves to through media and relationships. We may establish wise boundaries for daily living. We may submit to effective teaching to mold our thoughts and guide our words. We may pray. We may trust. Even so, our efforts cannot shield us from all heartache. When it does come—and it will—God has a plan to rescue us.

"And this is the reason: God lives forever and is holy.
He is high and lifted up.
He says, "I live in a high and holy place,
but I also live with people who are sad and humble.
I give new life to those who are humble
and to those whose hearts are broken."

— Isaiah 57:15 NCV

One day, I knew it was time to spread the word; the One who created us and calls our names wants to help us get beyond our past. He mends broken hearts without a complicated formula or difficult teaching. Would you like to join me? All that's required of you at this moment is a glimmer of hope and a fragment of faith to compel you to keep reading.

The One who created us and calls our names wants to help us get beyond our past.

When I began to write these words, I'd already been a part of life-changing prayer for emotional healing, but I decided to search through the Bible and read every scripture I could find with the word "heart." It was a quiet morning in my library, and I casually turned the pages to locate each verse. Each word I read entered my head and landed in my heart. God's character and His limitless love were evident, but remarkably, at the same time, a load of intense emotional pain piled into my chest. Aware of some memories I'd locked away for years, in a tearful few minutes, I prayed, and God exchanged the pain from my memories with tranquility. While I sat stunned by the unexpected experience, I imagined what the world would be like if everyone knew how God waits, eager to do the same for them.

Heartbreak in the Bible

Heartbreaking experiences go as far back as the beginning of man. In Genesis, the first book of the Bible, we learn the devastation Adam and Eve felt when, out of jealousy, their elder son murdered their younger son.

Let's take a moment to examine another time of heartbreak mentioned early in the Bible. For the first three months of Moses' life, his mother and father hid him from Pharaoh's soldiers (who were on order to kill all newly born Hebrew boys) (Exodus 1:22 and 2:1–3). How traumatic; what great measures they took to keep their young baby quiet and tucked away from the threat of death.

Then, when it was clear they could no longer successfully hide Moses, his mother, Jochebed, nursed him for what she felt would be the last time, snuggled him into a papyrus-reed basket, and kissed her beautiful son goodbye. Imagine her tears as she clutched her heart and released the basket into the dense reeds of the Nile. Despite her pain, she remained hopeful God would rescue her precious son.

And He did! We go on to read in Exodus 2:4–9:

> *"His sister stood at a distance to see what would happen to him. Then Pharaoh's daughter went down to the Nile to bathe, and her attendants were walking along the riverbank. She saw the basket among the reeds and sent her female slave to get it. She opened it and saw the baby. He was crying, and she felt sorry for him. 'This is one of the Hebrew babies,' she said.*
>
> *Then his sister asked Pharaoh's daughter, 'Shall I go and get one of the Hebrew women to nurse the baby for you?'*

'Yes, go,' she answered. So the girl went and got the baby's mother. Pharaoh's daughter said to her, 'Take this baby and nurse him for me, and I will pay you.' So the woman took the baby and nursed him ."

Miraculously, Jochebed became her own son's nursemaid, able to care for him under the safety of Pharaoh's daughter. Continuing to read the story of Moses, we learn his mother suffered heartbreak again as she gave him over to his benefactor when he was weaned. He would receive the care and attention of people she did not know and experience things she could not control.

Jochebed probably did not live to see Moses become the leader of the Hebrew nation. In time, after many trials, his life revealed the magnificent plan God had in place for him all along.

Some of you may feel you do not know God well, but you know heartbreak very well. Perhaps you are reading this book in search of hope.

We needn't look far to know of many other stories of heartache in the Bible. For that matter, we needn't look beyond our own mirrors to see pain and heartache. None of us is exempt.

Some of you may feel you do not know God well, but you know heartbreak very well. Perhaps you are reading this book in search of hope.

God knows you. He created you and loves you. He thought about you even *before* your birth. He has a plan for you!

> "Before I formed you in the womb I knew you."
>
> **— Jeremiah 1:5 NIV**

His plan includes the healing of painful memories stored in your heart. He knows of every anxious moment and has seen every tear fall. My prayer as you turn these pages is that your hope is ignited, your faith intensified, and your innermost being is healed.

Kim's Story

We met at Kim's home for lunch, talking about her experiences over the previous two years. As she described the trauma of an assault and robbery of almost everything dear to her, she panicked and began to hyperventilate. I knew these panic attacks happened frequently. After she calmed down, I asked if she would allow me to pray with her for healing from the trauma, confident in God's loving response.

With the soft sunlight streaming in on her tear-streaked face, placing her hand over her heart, she prayed a simple prayer. As we finished, she took a deep breath. Her slow smile was filled with peace. We thanked God for His faithful response. Never again has Kim suffered a panic attack from the assault and robbery.

Does she miss items stolen in the robbery? Yes, but the sting deep in her soul—what seized her, causing the panic attacks—was gone.

If you feel you do not know God well, or you doubt He would do the same for you, I promise God longs to be a part of your life. He's capable of much more than we can imagine. In just a few moments, He heals broken hearts and repairs wounded souls.

Others of you, already confident God is real, recognize the Father, the Son, and the Holy Spirit, are doing your best to abide by the guidelines for life found in the Bible. When crises come, you cry out to Him, wondering—*does He care enough? . . . is He powerful enough to carry me beyond this pain?*

His Word says:

"The Lord is close to the brokenhearted, and he saves those whose spirits have been crushed."

— Psalm 34:18 NCV

I am no stranger to trauma. My mother's illnesses, family divorces, personal failures, business losses, children's diseases, the death of loved ones, and even planned suicide are much too familiar. During the year of my most intense heartache, I hid behind a mask of courage and stayed strong throughout each day—except on Friday nights. That's when I would hide in the bathroom behind sounds of the shower and sob for a very long time, releasing all my pent-up agony for the week. No one knew.

Heartache and heartbreak piled one on another, but then, there's GOD. For every tragic occurrence—for every piercing wound in my soul—God carried me through. In time, He divinely healed the pain from each memory, gently replacing it with peace.

Does God have this same healing and resulting calm available to everyone? The resounding answer is: "Yes!" The reason? He created each person with plans for a relationship with Him. He loves us all, no matter what we've ever done and no matter what has been done to us. His love is unlimited and His peace is surprising.

For some of you, the heartbreak from your experiences may still be so raw you wonder if you'll ever breathe again. Perhaps not even from recent events, the pain persists affecting your thoughts, motivations, and actions. No one else knows it's there; but it sits buried deep in a secret closet, with a sign on the door marked "Brave and Strong."

He loves us all, no matter what we've ever done and no matter what has been done to us.

For those experiencing stress and heartache, please know this book is about HOPE and HEALING. It's about a simple prayer God responds to in a magnificent way.

There IS One who absolutely loves us—One we can count on to make the pain all better.

He is the Great Physician, Almighty God, Jehovah Rapha, who listens when we pray, and is certain to respond.

When we open our hearts and expose the pain, we can trust God to heal it.

The Bible is God's way of speaking to humanity, and prayer is humanity's way of speaking to God. On the following pages, you'll find lots of words God is saying to you, and you'll have plenty of opportunities to speak to Him.

The Bible is God's way of speaking to humanity, and prayer is humanity's way of speaking to God.

LET'S PRAY

"Dear Heavenly Father, I choose to believe I acquired this book for a reason. I believe You have a plan through this reading, which may alter my life. Please replace any anxiety I'm feeling now with hope for my healing. Please increase my faith and confidence in who You are and in how much You love me. Help me, Lord, to transfer the information I'm reading from my head and capture it in my heart. I pray my tomorrow does not have to be like my yesterday. In Jesus' name, I pray. Amen."

LET'S ASK

What would I ask the Lord to do for me while reading this book? Change my own life? Gain information to help others?

_____

_____

_____

_____

_____

_____

_____

_____

_____

_____

_____

_____

_____

_____

_____

_____

CHAPTER 2

A NEW NORMAL

WHAT IS IT ABOUT life experiences we cannot control that leave us broken and wounded? Sometimes it's impossible to see how we'll ever get to the other side of our pain. There are moments when our despair crushes our soul and breaks our spirit, but the more we learn about God, the better we understand, in the end, that His result is magnificent.

Losing the family business, my father's legacy, crushed us. We attempted every business improvement any of us could conceive. We made every operational change we could think of. We prayed every way we knew how. We submitted prayer requests to countless others. We fasted. Humiliation and grief weighed heavy with our disappointment and brokenness. We hurt. We really hurt.

Along our painful path, God provided for every need and eventually relocated us to a city where another journey was to begin. In spite of all the positives, I collected heart wounds that had not healed.

When I learned about heart healing, the memories associated with losing our business were some of the first I prayed about. God put an end to the suffocating feeling I had whenever I recalled that period. What a tremendous relief! He'll do the same for you.

Is the Lord touching a place deep within you, a place where your soul is scarred from hurtful events? Looking back, do you see unhealed wounds? Has it been normal for you to push those memories away? Usually we do our best to ignore the hurt, to pretend it isn't there. Much like a bomb that needs to be defused, ignored pain potentially explodes in other damaging ways, including anxiety, sickness, and sleeplessness.

There are answers, though. I just returned from a weekend event where hundreds of people—young, old, rich, poor, short, and tall—were prayed for individually, experienced profound heart healing, and exchanged pain from their past for more peaceful tomorrows.

***

Wounds come in all kinds of categories, and they leave a variety of marks on our souls. Recently, I was examining a picture I'd taken of twelve imperfect seashells I'd collected during a walk on the beach. That morning, I'd read a moving story in the Old Testament of the Bible (Joshua 3 and 4) when God performed a miracle for the Israelites. As they miraculously crossed the Jordan River to begin a new life, God instructed them to collect twelve stones representing each of the twelve tribes of Israel. The stones commemorated the event for God's people forever. Sensing that important changes were coming in my life with my husband, I wanted to collect twelve stones, too. Since stones weren't available, I searched for twelve seashells. The only ones I could find were damaged by the waves and wind.

Before taking the picture of the shells, I washed them, hopeful their look would improve in the light shining through the kitchen window. The cleaning and sunlight actually accentuated all the defects of the shells. Little did I know, these imperfections would have important meaning one day.

Now stroking my fingers across the old picture, it seemed I could feel the imperfections. Waves of irregular ridges ran across the exterior of one; another had holes all over; a few others had large pits; and in one, a deep crack trailed along the side. I was suddenly struck by the comparison of these shells to the variety of marks life leaves on our hearts. Some of us have waves of painful experiences, others experience stab after stab of hurtful moments, while others are left with one or two deep wounds or breaks from extreme trauma.

Imagine sitting in the midst of a great crowd of people—a shopping mall, a theme park, a ball game, or a movie theater. As you picture all the people surrounding you, ask God's Holy Spirit to show you the brokenness and despair hidden deep inside. The burdens and suffering may shock you. You might see family members dealing with divorce or disease, teenagers aching from bullying or ridicule, those worrying over a doctor's diagnosis, silent victims of abuse—the list goes on.

Are you weary of it all? God sees our deep, innermost secret suffering, hidden from the world. What has become normal to us is quietly exhausting us, causing anxiety, anger, and panic attacks, and is making us sick. He knows every moment in every life when the cruel words were spoken, or loved ones walked out, or horrible events happened. There are no secrets with God. We can't hide our pain from Him in that closet marked "Brave and Strong," and we can't stash it away in a fortress of numbness, and we can't bury it with alcohol, food, drugs, or shopping.

God sees. God knows. God loves. God heals.

What has become normal to us is quietly exhausting us, causing anxiety, anger, and panic attacks, and is making us sick.

Salt Shakers, iPods, and Such

I'd spent most days keeping the house perfectly neat for real-estate showings, so our final weeks in Texas brought a frenzy of online sales, yard sales, giveaways, and donations. Friends and family members arrived in shifts the last week, helping us sort and pack for our move to a house half the size. At about 10:00 p.m. on the intended day of our departure, my husband announced the full truck couldn't hold another item. Desperate to at last begin the long drive to California, in the final moments before we left, we bagged our remaining belongings, placing them on the front curb for passersby. I avoided looking at the patio furniture discarded in the driveway and the bagged treasures along the sidewalk. Tears quietly fell as we drove away at midnight.

Despite knowing we were meant to serve at the headquarters of an international ministry in Los Angeles, the move was difficult. We left most of our family, friends, and hearts in Texas, previously always our home.

Unpacking took great effort in our little California cottage—one box at a time—one salvaged treasure at a time. In the middle of one particular night, my eyes flew open, realizing I had not found our salt shaker. The old tin shaker was given to me by my grandmother over forty years earlier! Without recipes, I knew from experience just how many shakes each of our traditional family meals required. How would I ever manage without it? I cried again—and again.

It's just a salt shaker, I told myself. The real issue, though— the thing that gave me daily anxiety—was what the salt shaker represented. I would think of the shaker and of *all* the things I had left behind. That also prompted me to think of the life we'd left behind. In the big picture, they were hardly important, but I grieved over their loss. I struggled to get past my past.

My struggle over loss was very real, but when I finally grasped how to pray specifically for my own heartache, God did something amazing. He took away the pain and replaced it with peace! Although it started with the salt shaker, every time I thought of something lost which stirred up grief, I stopped to pray over the broken feeling for that item. Do I still miss my things? Yes, but gone are the anxiety attacks and pain from the trauma. Of far more value is the tremendous blessing of obeying God with the move to serve Him. Oh, and in time I acquired a similar, even better, salt shaker.

***

Having heard me speak at an event about "Heart Matters," a friend shared this story with me:

> *"Some years ago, I went on a mission trip to Turkey, Greece, and Bulgaria. I knew no one on the trip and had never traveled out of the country by myself. At the time, I also had a great fear of relationships with strangers. I hid behind my iPod—it had everything for me—my Bible, music, and even FaceTime so I could connect with my husband back in the States.*

"Stranded for a bit with the group on an island in Greece, I spent the time alone with my feet hanging over the pier. As I got up, my iPod decided to go fishing. I lost everything! I shared what I had lost with someone, and she immediately held a "memorial service" for my iPod, thanking it for the joy that it brought and mentioning the sadness at its loss, etc. That little bit of prayer she offered helped to heal my heart and also led to a friendship that crosses miles!

"You were right when you said it didn't take much time for God to heal your heart—but it does take intentionality in going to Him to address the issue!"

I'm grateful she remembered the talk and mentioned the importance of intentionality. Specific prayer brings profound results. We'll talk about this more very soon.

These attachments to objects certainly aren't as devastating as a huge list of other tragic events, but God will heal every experience of heartbreak. He never said He'd only heal the major wounds. He said He would heal the brokenhearted without any stipulation about the severity of the event. If you are thinking of a similar crisis in your life, please know it's as important to our Heavenly Father as any other agonizing event.

Collateral Damage

Without intervention from the Divine, it is challenging to avoid our own heartache when those dear to us suffer pain and trauma.

When our family lost our once-successful supermarket chain, hundreds of employees lost their jobs as well. Some were part of our supermarket family of friends for thirty years or more. Clearly, we were not the only ones who suffered over the loss. They and their families experienced pain and stress during that time as well. Together, we were all part of the collateral damage of losing the company.

This ripple effect of collateral damage, feeling others' hurt, may show itself in unexpected ways.

> ### *Without intervention from the Divine, it is challenging to avoid our own heartache when those dear to us suffer pain and trauma.*

Richard's Story

My friend Richard sent an email after he listened to my presentation of "Heart Matters" on the telephone. While listening to provide feedback to me about the material, he was affected personally. He wrote:

> *"Saturday, I heard you share about broken hearts. As I listened, I thought of my mom. She had all of the symptoms you described since my brother was*

killed years ago. Other painful events have happened in her life, but the death of my brother was the one that broke her heart severely. Listening to what you shared over the phone, a new desire entered my heart to speak to my mother.

"Suddenly, the Lord showed me I also had pain from my brother's death in my own heart. I, too, was brokenhearted, though not as severely as my mom.

"During that small conference you held over the phone, I felt the Lord heal my heart. I feel different! I would have never thought the words from the Bible 'and heal the brokenhearted' would affect me the way they did. The Lord showed me that verse was about me and for me.

"Thank you for having shared those words and for what the Lord has given you through this ministry for people like me. I needed to hear them and hadn't even realized it."

What verse was he referring to?

"He heals the brokenhearted
And binds up their wounds
[healing their pain and comforting their sorrow]."

— Psalm 147:3 AMP

The Lord gently mended years of Richard's grieving and buried heartache in a miraculous moment.

As with Richard, our pain may not be obvious to us, but that doesn't mean it isn't there. Heartache has many sources and shows itself in many ways. The extent of pain in this world is very broad, but the stroke of God's healing hand is supreme, and broader still.

> **The extent of pain in this world is very broad, but the stroke of God's healing hand is supreme, and broader still.**

* * *

This morning, I saw a news report of a motorcyclist thrown into the path of an oncoming 18-wheeler. The accident was witnessed by the victim's husband and fellow riders. Perhaps just a short time before, they'd all shared breakfast and a friendly conversation about the ride ahead. The husband, truck driver, friends, and first responders—all were in distress. What an abundance of heartbreak resulted from that accident!

Vicarious Trauma

Vicarious trauma is something that happens to caring people who are caring for people. It is also called "compassion fatigue" or "secondary traumatic stress." Usually, it refers to professionals who provide care to victims of trauma.

First responders, humanitarian workers, doctors, ministers, teachers, counselors, or just caring friends offering a listening ear to someone dear are all exposed to vicarious trauma. The effects of other people's sufferings and needs collect in the hearts of these compassionate people. Over time, they begin to suffer from their own form of trauma—vicarious trauma.

Imagine opening up our minds and our hearts to the worst in human experience on a regular basis. Ultimately, this can change the way we see ourselves and things that matter to us. If it alters our psychology, it can also alter our spiritual well-being. Our sense of purpose, hope, and faith all rest in our spirituality. It's important to be aware of this exposure to the impact of others' trauma.

Vicarious trauma is something that happens to caring people who are caring for people.

If you are a caring person who is caring for others, remember, God's healing is not just for them; it is for you as well.

"My soul is weary with sorrow;
strengthen me according to your word."

— Psalm 119:28 NIV

***

In many ministry settings, where victims of trauma or despair are prayed for, leaders are careful to end each gathering with a protective prayer for all those who served on ministry teams. This prayer shields them from taking on the heartbreak and any negative effects of those to whom they have ministered. Over the years, this was the format I was most often exposed to. Recently, I came to appreciate that protective prayer more than ever.

I had worked on this book for several weeks, writing about my own heartbreak and gathering the moving stories of others with whom I had prayed for heart healing. As a writer, it's important I dig deeply into my feelings and theirs, to convey the message well.

One morning, I awoke emotionally fragile. For the next few days, I cried over anything, and I mean *anything*! I examined what had otherwise become a peaceful life and asked God for clarity. I tried to shake off the emotions rattling around inside me, even taking an extra nap or two, thinking perhaps I was just overtired.

During this time in my research, I came across the term "vicarious trauma." Hello! I suddenly realized I was no longer covered by the prayers of leaders at ministry events. I was working alone on a project that dumped my feelings into a pressure cooker. With every story of abuse or disease—with each tale of someone's anguish—I heaped their suffering upon myself. My heart became filled with the pain of others.

It's important to state that with each person's story I'm referring to, God responded to prayer and healed each broken heart. I had still unknowingly taken on others' burdens because I was so emotionally connected to their experiences.

At that point, my own heart needed healing—again!

If you are a caregiver, a counselor, a minister, a first responder, someone in the medical profession, or anyone who witnesses the trauma and struggles of others, you especially risk unknowingly carrying their burdens. I applaud you. Your calling is difficult, but please remember that the results of your work, although significant, may also be causing you harm. In Chapter 6, you will find a prayer of covering and protection for anyone at risk of experiencing vicarious trauma.

* * *

Not one of us is exempt from heartache. Whatever the source of the hurt, we may:

- Push the painful thoughts into a closet deep within our souls.
- Add another brick to the wall around our hearts for protection.
- Act like we don't care or it isn't affecting us.
- Self-medicate with the chocolate in the pantry or the beer in the fridge or the antidepressant in the cabinet or the tempting purchase.
- Overachieve to bury our pain under accomplishments.
- Shut down and withdraw.

Ultimately, we must face the reality that these steps will not bring healing; they only suppress the pain, which will resurface another day.

Whatever we do to bury it, stuff it, medicate it, control it, or ignore it, all of the awful stuck-in-your-gut pain explodes in a list of symptoms. Not one of us escapes the harmful effects of memories that leave our souls fractured and torn.

No matter what you have experienced—
no matter how little hope you have felt in
the past—our Creator has a plan for you.
As He heals the broken places within you,
more of His map for your life is revealed.
Little by little, step by step, He engineers
your circumstances and navigates the way.
Just throw some faith into your backpack
of belief to make the trip with Him.

Whether you've been bullied or abandoned, rejected, abused, or shamed; whether you've experienced loss, collateral damage, or vicarious trauma—whatever the reason for your hurt, God is ready to repair your heart and recalibrate your life.

No matter what you have experienced—no matter how little hope you have felt in the past—our Creator has a plan for you. As He heals the broken places within you, more of His map for your life is revealed. Little by little, step by step, He engineers your circumstances and navigates the way. Just throw some faith into your backpack of belief to make the trip with Him.

Is recalling a painful memory causing pressure in your own heart right now? If so, let's press a "pause" button on the pain. Placing your hand over your (physical) heart, let's ask the Lord to calm you as you continue reading. Soon, we'll be praying for healing, and you will be different, too!

Your "normal" is about to change.

LET'S PRAY

"Lord Jesus, I ask that You calm my soul and my spirit right now. Please come to my heart and give me a quiet knowledge that your healing is coming. Amen."

Close your eyes, take a deep breath, pause, smile, and trust. If you question your existence, or your days are full of torment from the past, know that there is One who gave up His life for you. He wants you to know you have value and He offers hope, healing, and freedom to you. He's waiting to help you. He is able.

> "Who has gone up to heaven and come down?
> Whose hands have gathered up the wind?
> Who has wrapped up the waters in a cloak?
> Who has established all the ends of the earth?
> What is his name, and what is the name of his son?
> Surely you know!
> "Every word of God is flawless;
> he is a shield to those who take refuge in him."
>
> **— Proverbs 30:4-5 NIV**

***

LET'S ASK

As I've read this chapter, how has the Lord spoken to me? Did an event wound me so deeply, it seemed to tattoo "hurt" on my soul forever?

_____

_____

_____

_____

_____

_____

_____

_____

_____

Am I ready to ask the Lord to remove the distressing part of that experience, but keep the memory if He chooses to use it for my good or the good of others?

_____

_____

_____

In my own words, I ask God to heal me as I turn the pages of this book:

_____

_____

_____

_____

_____

_____

_____

_____

_____

_____

_____

_____

_____

_____

_____

_____

_____

_____

CHAPTER 3

HOBBLED

IT WAS SUPPOSED TO be a working vacation. If I could just finish this intense work schedule, I'd soon lounge on the hotel veranda and pound out a chapter or two of the book. Every day I focused on deadlines while household chores and packing haunted me. My over-functioning body's response to each morning's alarm was, "Nooo!" The exhaustion was my fault. I kept my eyes on self-imposed goals and ignored the mysterious chest pains tracking down my arms.

Within days of our arrival in Mexico, I injured my shoulder in a fall and my tired body came down with the flu. There I lay in my hotel room with a fever, an aching shoulder, no TV, no good books (because I thought I'd be writing) and a computer that had just crashed. Confined, I thought and prayed for the five remaining days of the trip. That's when the word "hobbled" came to mind.

I remembered when trainers hobble a horse, his legs are tied to restrain and teach him. When I looked up the definition of "hobbled," I learned hobbling is designed to slow the movement or action of something or someone. Yes, clearly, I was hobbled.

I knew I needed rest, but that goes against my nature. Meeting deadlines is fulfilling for me, but I tend to set too many, too often, and too soon. Now hobbled—unable to connect with anyone in any way—I realized God could finally keep me from over-functioning. His purpose? It was time for serious rest, not work, and I sure got it. This injury and illness and the subsequent recovery time provided more thoughtful rest than I'd had in years.

God releases the bonds that hobble us and He gently moves us forward to accomplish the purposes He has for us.

As my body recovered, my mind turned toward God's priorities and the peace only He can provide. My pre-vacation chest pains disappeared, my shoulder grew stronger, and my energy restored while my relationship with the Lord grew deeper. I later read that hobbling horses enables them to have peace and be calm when they experience a crisis. Interesting . . .

I read on a horse-lovers' forum that hobbling, though intended for good, may in fact cause harm. A horse in danger—let's say tangled in barbed wire—learned from hobbling to stay still and wait for help. If help never comes, the horse likely will never move, staying quietly tangled and trapped.

When our hearts hurt and break—when we experience disappointment, depression, despair—we may become hobbled, too. God does not design this faulted hobbling, which prevents us from moving forward with the purposes He has for us. We're stuck—our emotional maturity and growth can be stunted at the point when the pain was inflicted, with subtle bonds that weave their damaging way through our souls.

- Is a lengthy period of grief holding you back?
- Did a job layoff cause you to doubt your future?
- Are you reliving a tragic event in your mind over and over again?
- Are you lonely without being alone?
- Did abuse destroy your dignity or rob you of self-worth?

God will rescue you. His word assures us:

> "The LORD is close to the brokenhearted
> and saves those who are crushed in spirit"
> **— Psalm 34:18 NIV**

God releases the bonds that hobble us and He gently moves us forward to accomplish the purposes He has for us.

Claudia's Story

It was their twenty-eighth wedding anniversary, and Claudia pushed her husband's caressing hand away from hers. "Sometimes I don't feel like you love me," she said.

"Claudia," he replied, "I don't understand why you say that! You are the love of my life."

When she told me this story, she added, "And sometimes I don't feel like God loves me, either. The feeling comes and goes. I wish I could take what I know about His love for me and push it down from my head into my heart. Somehow it just doesn't get there."

Knowing our relationship with our earthly father can impact our acceptance of a relationship with our Heavenly Father, I asked, "What was your relationship with your dad like?"

"Well," she said, "When my mother was pregnant with me, my father denied I was his. Eventually, he accepted I was his and would show up to spend a little time with me. Soon he'd leave, and I wouldn't see him again for a long time."

"With all that inconsistency, it was hard to trust that he loved you, wasn't it? Do you think that has affected your ability to believe in God's consistent love? To take it a step further, perhaps those flawed beliefs have crippled your ability to accept your husband's love, too."

She cried with recognition of the truth. Each time her father's random visits ended, little Claudia wondered if he'd ever return. She was conditioned to feel unsure and unworthy.

We prayed first for the Lord to heal all the places inside her crushed by the dysfunctional love of her dad, and then we asked the Lord to transfer her head knowledge of God's love and her husband's love to her heart. God swiftly answered our prayers and changed her life and her marriage. In just ten minutes, He removed what had been hobbling their marriage for twenty-eight years, and gently healed Claudia's wounds.

Ken's Story

As a little boy, Ken recognized the disappointed looks from his father. He tried hard to play baseball, football, and golf as his dad once did. His father's criticism stamped the word "failure" on Ken's heart. He didn't consciously accept that label, but he subconsciously lived it day after day for over sixty years.

As this talented man strived to feel successful, any degree of failure resulted in frustration and anxiety. Even at the slightest misstep, like spilling milk, he became angry over his clumsiness. Aside from a moment of exceptional confidence he experienced in college, Ken generally felt he couldn't do anything right. Unable to quickly learn a new software feature, he slammed pads on his desk and stomped out of the room. At his boss's guidance and correction, he felt offended and resentful. Unknowingly, he was hobbled by his past. Ken's pain from consistently disappointing his father affected his belief in himself. Ken continuously criticized himself, in large things and small, from childhood on—until one fateful day when he was seventy years old.

On that day, he prayed for God to heal his heart from the crushing memories with his father. At the end of the short prayer, Ken recalled that confident moment he experienced in college, and he felt a similar feeling return. God untangled his bond to failure and replaced it with new confidence in the unconditional love of God the Father.

Shortly afterward, Ken's wife relayed an interesting event. While she prepared dinner one evening, he bumped into her, knocking spaghetti on the floor. She waited for the usual explosive reaction. Instead of slamming his fist onto the kitchen counter, he calmly apologized and cleaned up the spaghetti as she stood stunned. He soon learned new features of his business software with ease, and his relationship with his demanding employer was totally redefined. He reports he's in a place of peace instead of constant strife.

Father God's response to Ken's prayer was immediate; the results appeared consistently in everyday ways over time. Only God could alter a man's perception of himself and others so miraculously within a few minutes.

Evidence of Hobbling

How many times have we heard ourselves say about others:

- "Why don't they just get over it?"
- "She needs to move on with her life."
- "He'll never change."
- "Why doesn't he just stop drinking?"

Perhaps before we start to talk about others and their behaviors, let's consider that maybe they just can't get past their past. Perhaps these people have a roadblock on the superhighway between their heads and their hearts. They hear God loves them, but this knowledge of love has not yet traveled to the place of replacing the pain in their hearts—the pain affecting their will, emotions, motivations, thoughts, and actions.

Perhaps before we start to talk about others and their behaviors, let's consider that maybe they just can't get past their past.

* * *

For over forty years, I struggled with saying "Goodbye." No matter who, I would get so emotional I would have to walk away to compose myself. Whether our kids came from college for the weekend, or guests left after a short visit, I would cry almost uncontrollably as they drove away. Seeing TV characters bid farewell even prompted tears. Airports were a big challenge. As I witnessed loved ones saying their goodbyes to their families, I struggled to hold back sobs. Let's just say it got a little embarrassing. Trying to shrug it off, my family decided it was just the way I was. When I created a scene, though, the unwanted drama disturbed me.

After one particularly troublesome experience, I decided I'd had enough. Why couldn't I get this under control? Why couldn't I just get over it?

I put my hand on my chest, looked heavenward, and asked, "What is going on, Lord? Why do I cry so deeply over goodbyes?" When His answer came, so powerful and clear, it weakened my knees.

Whether your heart wounds trace back four days or forty years, God awaits, ready to heal you by restoring the brokenness within you.

Remember my opening story in Chapter One. At fourteen years old, with no real understanding of the situation, we children listened behind a wall while our mother was whisked away to a psychiatric hospital for several months. When I was fifteen years old, she suffered a relapse. Because she was taken away while I was in school, I returned to an empty house once again.

Now, decades later, tears flowed as I remembered. Both times, Mom was gone without warning—both times, I had no chance to say "Goodbye."

I placed my hand over my heart and prayed a simple prayer for healing. The same Creator of the Universe, who formed me in my mother's womb, who blessed me with this caring mom, heard my cry and answered me.

Pain, long hidden in my heart's closet labeled "Brave and Strong," emerged that day. This time, I cried all of my goodbyes out in memory of my mom, while God removed the pain and allowed me to finally, finally, finally be at peace with this. I could get on with my life. No more embarrassing farewells and no more unreasonable reactions to others' goodbyes.

Whether your heart wounds trace back four days or forty years, God awaits, ready to heal you by restoring the brokenness within you. He'll also remove barriers to the future He desires for you. Your connection to that painful memory will no longer hobble you. Ask the Lord. Your life will begin to change.

Today you know your tomorrow does not have to be like your yesterday!

Bianca's Story

Bianca's parents sought their pastor's help. Her sixteenth birthday approached, with expected plans for her to wear a tiara to honor her and to show she was their "princess." Instead of expressing delight, she panicked. Increasing tension led to her disclosure of rape by a family friend years earlier. Under threat of harm to her family, she'd lived with this secret. Her shame made her feel unworthy of a crown. More than that, her revelation of this terrible secret rocked her emotional stability and devastated her parents.

Fortunately, this pastor knew what to do. Through his own experiences and training for heart healing, he'd acquired the knowledge and sensitivity to the Holy Spirit to pray with Bianca and her parents. Once she realized she in no way brought about the rape, and understood how much the Lord loved her, she could accept healing for the crushing experience years earlier. Bianca's face glowed. Imagine her parents' delight when she ran to her room and returned with the tiara crowning her head! There was much rejoicing in their home that night.

> "They will call to me, and I will answer them.
> I will be with them in trouble;
> I will rescue them and honor them."
>
> **— Psalm 91:15 NCV**

I think of the hundreds of victims of abuse with whom I have prayed. Most of the time, they've kept their secret for years, and they finally discover they can trust God enough to be vulnerable. They open their hearts and allow Him to heal them. In the pages to come, I will show you how.

> "My flesh and my heart may fail,
> but God is the strength of my heart
> and my portion forever."
>
> **— Psalm 73:26 NIV**

What in your past hobbles you? What keeps you from all the Lord has planned for you?

- Are you still grieving over a lost love, unable to move forward in life?
- Did that job loss cripple your ability to believe in yourself again?
- Are you emotionally tied to an event in your past?

It's possible you hadn't made the connection between your behavior and the wounding memory coming to mind. Nothing is coincidental. Perhaps you were meant to read this chapter to remind you of heartache holding you back. Good is on its way. God is on His way.

> "Peace I leave with you; my peace I give you.
> I do not give to you as the world gives.
> Do not let your hearts be troubled and do not
> be afraid."
>
> **— John 14:27 NIV**

Finally, no matter how you feel at this moment, God has a purpose in your pain. Although hard to hear and accept in the middle of suffering, know there is a map laid out for your life, and He has control of the GPS system. As He unlocks the hobbling hold on your past, your life will reroute toward the greater significance for which He created you!

As He unlocks the hobbling hold on your past, your life will reroute toward the greater significance for which He created you!

***

LET'S ASK

What experience hobbles me?

_____

_____

_____

_____

_____

_____

_____

_____

_____

_____

_____

_____

_____

_____

_____

_____

_____

If unsure, continue with the prayer below and add your notes here:

_____

_____

_____

_____

_____

_____

_____

_____

_____

LET'S PRAY

"Lord, I don't want to be held back by my past. I want my thoughts and actions to line up with the full life you intend for me. Please bring to my mind anything you want me to pray about that is hobbling me. Thank you for the answers that come.

I look forward to a future with greater purpose than ever before. Amen."

CHAPTER 4

RENEWAL

STABBING PAINS AND SEARING SCARS from our past can't be reasoned away nor shoved into a hidden place without putting our health at risk. Whether hurt from a long-ago event, a sudden experience, or a series of circumstances, the impact may show up in a variety of symptoms. Why? The hurts simmer deep within our souls, eventually boiling over, toppling their effects like dominoes from our brains throughout our bodies.

Angelique's Story

Late one morning, I had an overwhelming sense to call my friend, Angelique. We hadn't spoken in over a year, but it seemed we could always connect as though we had communicated every day. In recent years, trauma had trounced on her life, so I had tender thoughts over checking in with her again. She was still in bed when I called. I discovered she'd been there for months. Chronic fatigue and various other maladies required a table top of medications and crippled her lifestyle.

> *The more we learn about how much God loves us and is reliable to do what He says He will do, the more we allow Him to reset our hearts toward peace. The more peace we have, the better health we experience.*

Angelique knew the Lord well, but she couldn't climb out of her downward spiral. Her weakened voice confirmed she needed God to reach down from heaven to rescue her! Wholeheartedly, this sweet friend joined me in prayer.

"Oh, I feel so much better," she said as we ended our conversation. Her voice sounded more energized. What a loving God who calls us to uplift and support each other!

When I touched base a month or two after we prayed, she was out of bed much of the time and increasingly active. What a thrill to hear the details of her recovery. A few months later, I received a card from her with this message:

"Just a quick note to let you know what God has done along with your prayers. In January, there was a significant breakthrough in my health issues. Since then I have had few symptoms, have been able to engage in more activities, and have been sleeping better than I have for years.

Thank you for healing prayers, and praise to God, the Ultimate Healer."

—*Angelique*

* * *

The more we learn about how much God loves us and is reliable to do what He says He will do, the more we allow Him to reset our hearts toward peace. The more peace we have, the better health we experience.

Since Scripture is God's way of speaking to us, we want to give these words particular notice:

> "My son, pay attention to what I say;
> turn your ear to my words.
> Do not let them out of your sight,
> keep them within your heart;
> for they are life to those who find them
> and health to one's whole body."

— Proverbs 4:20-22 NIV

So, if we listen to the things God says to us in the Bible, and keep these words in our hearts, they will give life and health to our whole bodies.

He says He will heal the brokenhearted and the crushed in spirit. Now, we just need to know how to allow Him to do so; how to open our hearts to Him and ask Him for our personal miracles. Imagine with me what could happen if, around the world, broken hearts were mended by God, and the cause of much of our sicknesses miraculously avoided.

About Stress

A high percentage of health issues are related to stress. People may follow programs with proper diet, exercise, and medical attention, but if the stress in their lives is not resolved, there is still very real danger to their health and well-being.

Trauma and heartache are breeding grounds for stress.

Acute stress has a beginning and an end. Typically I'm able to avoid the Los Angeles freeways during rush hour, but when I know I have to hit I-405 on a Friday at 4:00 p.m., I get anxious hours earlier. That anxiety stays with me until I return home again, but the stressful experience does come to an end and all is well again. There was a beginning to the stress when I first learned the trip was necessary, and there was an end to the stress when I returned home again.

Trauma and heartache are breeding grounds for stress.

Chronic stress never seems to leave us. Unresolved effects of trauma and heartbreak fuel chronic stress. Even when a painful memory is tucked away in our hidden heart closet, the anxiety hovers quietly within, impacting our physiology far more than we may realize.

Then, there's God . . .

Camille's Story

Camille, one of those friends others turn to in times of need, is well known for her ability to encourage others. I imagine God leans close to listen to her prayers. She's the first person I called the morning I realized I was to write this book. I expected words of wise instruction from her. Instead, after hearing the purpose of the book, she asked me to pray.

"I know why we're having this conversation," she said. "I have never allowed myself to grieve over [my husband's] death. He passed away three years ago this week, and I recognize I'm paying a price for holding my emotions inside. Before he died, we were able to say goodbye and I knew he was with God. I thought I should be happy for him but have not allowed myself to cry once since he died."

A year after her husband died, she was diagnosed with breast cancer. Because she had not released her grief, and was then coping with cancer, we knew it was time to ask God our Healer to bring her peace and comfort.

I gulped back the nervous grip on my throat. Who was I to pray with this amazing woman? She was in Texas, and I was in California, yet God, who can be in all places at all times, doesn't let a little distance keep Him from performing miracles.

We prayed. God responded and opened the gate which had held back the hot tears hidden within her. For one thousand and ninety-five days, she had locked up her emotions. With her final sniffles, she announced, "I feel like a new car driven off the lot!" We shared a lot of tearful laughing, and added a request that the Lord would also heal her of the infirmity connected to her grief. Since our prayer, the cancer is no longer active, and she is recovering her vitality. Only God could do this.

What does God's Word say about the connection between our thoughts and our health?

> "Dear friend, I pray that you may enjoy good health
> and that all may go well with you,
> even as your soul is getting along well."
>
> — 3 John 2 NIV

***

The Motown classic recorded by Jimmy Ruffin and released in 1966, "What Becomes of the Brokenhearted?" has been dancing around in my head for days. What does become of the brokenhearted?

One day, I noticed a story aired on television about Broken Heart Syndrome (Takotsubo Cardiomyopathy or Stress

Cardiomyopathy.)[1] "The theory is that an event triggers the brain to signal the adrenal glands, which in turn send stress hormones that make the heart go haywire." Broken Heart Syndrome occurs more often in women but causes more fatalities in men. Victims may be otherwise healthy and commonly have open, unblocked arteries. Sudden shock and stress appear to be the sources of the syndrome.

This syndrome is often blamed when long-term couples die within a short time of each other. When someone dear to us passes away, we become vulnerable because of our body's reaction to stress.

I remember hearing of a couple whose son was tragically murdered while attending college away from home. The grieving parents did their best to cope through the shocking reality of their son's death. One morning, about a year after the murder, the parents said their goodbyes to each other as they headed to their respective jobs. Not long after the wife arrived at her workplace, she received a call that her husband had suddenly passed away. Doctors later told her he died of a broken heart.

Fortunately, only a small number of broken hearts end in death. Although not all extreme stresses or traumas cause Broken Heart Syndrome, they may rob us of the health and well-being God intended for us. They may steal our peace and ambush our joy. They distract us by our circumstances and keep us from fully trusting God with our future.

Sandy's Story

Sandy approached me at an event. "I heard you speak about heart healing a few months ago. I have to tell you when I first heard your message I thought to myself, *I've been a Christian for 42 years, and I've never heard that before. I'm going to have to pray about this and do some research.*

"But after you finished speaking, you had us turn to a partner to pray together for our hearts to be healed. A few weeks earlier, I was rejected by people whom I thought loved me and appreciated my efforts in their ministries. I was devastated! It was this memory of rejection I immediately recalled as my partner and I began to pray.

"I put my hand over my heart, and when my friend prayed, my physical heart began to vibrate! I have a very strong heart, and it makes no sense that it would suddenly do that. Then, as she spoke the prayer for my heart healing, I felt peace and the vibrating stopped!"

Sandy then began to smile and said it had been three months since their prayer for heart healing and none of the related anxiety had ever returned. She experienced a miracle moment. Though she had questioned the process, she trusted God, and He came through for her.

***

Post Traumatic Stress Disorder (PTSD)

Recently, I watched a miniseries on the Civil War. In a hospital scene, a soldier appeared to have a panic attack.

The observing doctor turned to his nurse and said, "He has Soldier's Heart."

I soon learned that the term "Soldier's Heart" comes from observations of soldiers returning from battle whose cardio-vascular systems were altered. Noticeable changes occurred in their heart dynamics, including their blood pressure and pulse rate.[2]

No heartache is too great nor too insignificant for His touch.

The original diagnosis of Soldier's Heart in the Civil War evolved to the label of "Shell Shock" in World War I and eventually to the most current label of "Post Traumatic Stress Disorder" (PTSD). Combat military personnel are not the only people susceptible to PTSD. It strikes many people who didn't go to war but have fought intense battles of the mind and body due to trauma.

This morning, I read a report from a Christian leader in the Middle East, where believers in Christ are persecuted relentlessly. Their level of stress and PTSD is beyond what many of us can comprehend; however, the reach of God's healing power is limitless. He comforts and heals the bro-kenhearted in any part of Creation. No heartache is too great nor too insignificant for His touch.

First Responders

First responders are trained to assist others when responding to an emergency. Doctors, policemen, firemen,

EMT's, etc. are prepared to help others in times of crisis, but who is ready to help them heal from the impact of their own trauma from these experiences?

Tom, retired from two branches of the military as well as police service, informed me veterans and first responders are unlikely to report symptoms of PTSD or to seek help because they fear being considered weak or unprofessional.

"We'd see horrors we couldn't talk to anyone about. The system for support is flawed. As a policeman, if a psychologist was sent to counsel us after a crisis, we knew any expression of weakness would be reported to the authorities over us. In a society filled with litigation, agencies can't risk employing first responders who could be considered a liability. We'd lose our jobs. We'd lose our homes. We'd lose our families. The risks were too great.

"Then, we'd go home and our wives would ask, 'How was your day, Honey?' What were we supposed to say? 'Well, I held a dying girl in my arms as she took her last breath. I responded to a domestic-violence call and was shot at. Oh, and I was involved in a car chase down the freeway.' What good would it do to dump the day on our wives? So, all the painful memories were locked inside us."

By avoiding discussions of their traumatic experiences, first responders may regularly add new painful memories deep into those heart closets marked "Brave and Strong."

Numerous studies confirm a clear association with PTSD for veterans and active duty personnel, first responders, and many men, women, and children who struggle with the effects of severe trauma. Those diagnosed with PTSD usually carry a number of other physical health problems that those who do not have PTSD don't have.[3]

> *Just because you don't let yourself think about your experiences, doesn't mean they aren't affecting you. May God compensate you for your sacrifice of service and replace each painful memory with improving health and increasing peace.*
> *Help is near. God is near.*

Stories that Can't be Told

Many stories from first responders and veterans cannot be told. The details remain locked away in the hearts of those who experienced them. I think of the veteran I once knew whose assignment was picking up remaining body parts after battles were over. Time and again, this young soldier suffered tremendous emotional trauma. The memories were too brutal and could not be allowed past the locked door in his heart. Few knew the reality of his experiences.

If you are struggling with PTSD or you are a first responder who has stashed away the awfulness of life in hidden places, you may have loud thoughts right now saying, "No! Don't think about it. Don't let the pain be exposed." Above the noise in your mind, God's voice is saying to you, "It's time. You're safe. I will heal your heart and restore your health. I am able."

Just because you don't let yourself think about your experiences, doesn't mean they aren't affecting you. May God compensate you for your sacrifice of service and replace each painful memory with improving health and increasing peace. Help is near. God is near.

***

The choice to open yourself to Him and pray is the most courageous work you'll do. God does the rest.

If you listen to the news, you know we live in a broken world filled with hurting people. It's easy to conclude that few of us escape the harmful effects of painful memories, which leave our souls fractured and broken. Each day, though, believers in God discover ways to reset painful experiences and the related memories.

- Do you struggle with a business loss?
- Does the image of your dying loved one pierce your soul?
- Did that one devastating remark crush your spirit?
- Is trauma preventing your joy and robbing you of good health?

Imagine getting permanent closure on these issues. How many people have told you just to think about the pain differently—reprogram your mind—talk to yourself with positivity? Perhaps you've advised others this way. In the end, this self-dependent process brings limited results. God's ways—higher and wiser—bring complete and certain healing.

Right now, you may doubt God can or would do such a thing for you. Perhaps He placed this book in your hands, speaking into your life, "It's time."

> "Then the word of the Lord came to Jeremiah:
> 'I am the Lord, the God of all mankind.
> Is anything too hard for me?'"
>
> **— Jeremiah 32:26-27 NIV**

When we pray together in the next chapter, we'll ask the Lord to end any connection between your stress and heartache to ailments, diseases, and issues of the mind and body. As He ends that connection, we will ask God to renew (meaning "make new again") your mind and your body.

Almighty God—the Creator of the Universe—He who loves all mankind, is ready and very willing to come to you and heal the painful memories affecting your life. When He does so, He will begin healing any physiological connections to the stress and trauma. When the hurting memory comes to mind, you will choose to either pack the wound back into the hidden places of your heart or pray for peace to replace it—pack it away or pray it away. The choice to open yourself to Him and pray is the most courageous work you'll do. God does the rest.

"Go back and tell Hezekiah, the ruler of my people,
'This is what the Lord, the God of your father David, says:
I have heard your prayer and seen your tears;
I will heal you . . .'"

— 2 Kings 20:5 NIV

This healing is not dependent upon your good works or your resilience. No matter your station in life, your age, or your gender, you are not exempt from heart wounds. Soon you will see that in a matter of moments, God will reconcile your past and clear the path for your future. When we pray, we will ask God for renewal as He heals any damage to your mind and body related to your heartache.

"You are made well because you believed.
Go in peace; be healed of your disease."

— Mark 5:34 NCV

LET'S ASK

After reading this chapter, do I remember a stressful time
when sickness or ill health followed?

_____

_____

_____

_____

_____

_____

_____

Have I sensed experiencing sickness as a result of current
heartache? If so, my thoughts:

_____

_____

_____

_____

_____

_____

_____

LET'S PRAY

Lord God, you already know what's going on inside of me. You know about everything that has wounded me in my past and You know about any physical, chemical, or emotional struggles I have that may be connected to these memories. Thank You for the hope you give me. Please give me faith that You can free everyone from the harmful effects of a painful past and help me trust that You will do it for me. Amen.

CHAPTER 5

HOPE FOR ALL

This imaginary story is based on biblical facts; it's a story of a woman seeking help from a life of despair.

S O WEAK. SO DESPERATE. So alone. Her sickness was considered unclean. For twelve long years, friends kept their distance, and family members were scarce. She tried doctor after doctor and spent all she had, yet no one could stop the unexplained bleeding.

From the window of her home, she stared at the shore of the Sea of Galilee and wondered if her life would ever be different. As others passed by, she longed for the relationships she once knew.

"I have news!" Her sister urgently called to her from outside her window.

"One has come to town who has healed many people. His name is Jesus, and they call him The Messiah. Miracles are happening all around him. You must go to see him, sister!"

Hope. The unfamiliar feeling ignited inside her. Could it be that this man, this miracle worker, could finally help? The possibility overwhelmed her but provided a burst of needed energy to go.

It seemed thousands were there when she arrived. With clothing wrapped carefully to protect her identity, hope pushed her through the tight crowds. Not far away was the man of whom her sister spoke of. Faith filled her when she saw Him and she knew.

"This is The One. If I can even touch his cloak, I know I'll be healed."

Just then, Jesus turned to walk away. *"Hurry!"* she urged herself. *"Catch up and touch him. Now! Now!"*

She lunged forward and touched the fringe on the hem of his garment. Suddenly, a surge of warmth flowed through her and brought the forgotten sensation of health and well-being. Stunned, she stopped short and let the crowd envelop her.

Feeling power leave Him, Jesus turned, inquiring who

had touched Him. She fell at his feet, trembling. "It was I, Lord. I knew if I could but touch your clothing, I'd be healed." Through her grateful tears, she saw His face, His gentle, understanding eyes. She saw love.

Jesus said to her, "Dear woman, you are made well because you believed. Go in peace; be healed of your disease."

(Based on Mark 5:25-34)

***

At times when we feel suspended somewhere between heartbreak and healing, we are strengthened by hope. That hope is someone loves us enough, and is powerful enough, to make our lives all better.

Just as the woman with the issue of blood, we are drawn to God by hope—hope that He has answers for our hurting hearts. Our hope will soon be followed by faith as God reconciles our past and unlocks our future—in miracle moments!

Before we talk about how we'll pray, it's important to focus on to Whom we are praying.

"You are worthy, our Lord and God,
to receive glory and honor and power,
for you created all things,
and by your will they were created
and have their being."

— Revelation 4:11 NIV

"Look up to the skies. Who created all these stars?

He leads out the army of heaven one by one and
calls all the stars by name.

Because he is strong and powerful,
not one of them is missing."

— Isaiah 40:26 NCV

"He says, 'Be still, and know that I am God.'"

— Psalm 46:10 NIV

God's work is flawless. His plans are limitless and perfect. He created all things, and He loves all of humanity; even those who do not yet know Him or His love. God is:

- **Loving** – giving freely; without conditions
- **Merciful** – kind, compassionate, forgiving
- **Gracious** – loving even though we don't deserve it or don't return love to Him
- **All-knowing** – aware of every detail
- **Supreme** – our Creator and Sovereign God, the greatest Being in the universe

When we choose to believe in Him in our lives—turning our eyes to Him for direction, hope and healing, He uses His power, from the farthest points of creation, to assist us and to engineer the direction and circumstances of our lives for great good.

Anywhere at any time, and everywhere all of the time, He is timeless. He is GOD.

When we choose to believe in Him in our lives—turning our eyes to Him for direction, hope and healing, He uses His power, from the farthest points of creation, to assist us and to engineer the direction and circumstances of our lives for great good.

> "For I know the plans I have for you," declares the Lord,
> "plans to prosper you and not to harm you,
> plans to give you hope and a future.
> Then you will call on me and come and
> pray to me, and I will listen to you.
> You will seek me and find me when
> you seek me with all your heart."
>
> **— Jeremiah 29:11-13 NIV**

***

By my mid-twenties, I found myself divorced and a single mother of two young daughters. I thought I could handle things on my own. So much for that. My life was a mess. I was confident I didn't need any rules and laws to follow; certainly not from a God who was up on His throne judging me.

I began attending some meetings, though, where others told me a different view of who God was. Paying particular attention to words about His love for me no matter what

I'd done, I wondered if what they were saying was true. One especially miserable night, over and over I examined the awful things I'd done, and the horrible things done to me. I decided it was worth a try to see what God could do.

He knew the awful things I'd done and the horrible things done to me, but He loved me anyway. Love, just pure love. He feels the same way about you.

While in bed, staring at the ceiling fan spinning slowly in the dim light, I said, "God, if what everyone is telling me about You is true, then I want that. Come into my life and change me. I admit I've made a mess of everything and I need a fresh start."

It was hardly a holy prayer, but it was from my heart; and I just knew He heard me. It was my first experience in knowing that even simple prayers bring magnificent responses.

In the following months, I learned more and more about Jesus. I'd always heard His story, being born in a manger and dying on a cross, but steadily I grew from knowing His story to knowing Him!

I learned Jesus, God in human form, chose to live a physical life on earth, but His thoughts and His ways were (and always will be) undeniably God. The life He lived here was lived with you and me in mind. He knew the awful things I'd done and the horrible things done to me, but He loved me anyway. Love, just pure love. He feels the same way about you.

There were moments I imagined Him sitting comfortably in a cozy room with me, a cup of coffee in hand, saying, "I know about all you've been thinking. Believe I am God. Admit your wrongs. Ask, and I will forgive that part of your history. Then, I will forget you ever made those poor choices at all."

The term for this—*justification*—means it's just as if we'd never committed the wrong.

> "Therefore, if anyone is in Christ,
> the new creation has come:
> The old has gone, the new is here!"
>
> **— 2 Corinthians 5:17 NIV**

I learned His love for us is extraordinary. Jesus came to Earth to stand in for us. As a willing substitute, He assumed responsibility for all the sins we ever committed—and ever would commit. He made this sacrifice for us for free. No charge. We just choose to believe, ask forgiveness, and invite Him to lead us.

> "But when [in God's plan] the proper time had fully come,
> God sent His Son, born of a woman, born under the
> [regulations of the] Law, so that He might redeem *and*
> liberate those who were under the Law, that we [who
> believe] might be adopted as sons [as God's children with all
> rights as fully grown members of a family]."
>
> **— Galatians 4:4-5 AMP**

And, those awful things done to us? Those cuts and bruises inside of us? Through His sacrifice, we will be healed. He'll show us the way.

He assumed responsibility for all the sins we ever committed—and ever would commit. He made this sacrifice for us for free. No charge.

Another Step

Jesus said:

"I am the door,
and the person who enters through me will be saved
and will be able to come in and go out and find pasture.
A thief comes to steal and kill and destroy,
but I came to give life—life in all its fullness."

— John 10:9-10 NCV

Are you ready for the extraordinary life God designed for you? Although He may not suddenly grant every request for material possessions you've always wanted, He will orchestrate the circumstances of your life from this moment on for great good. When trials come (as they do for all of us), He will provide hope, strength, understanding, and healing.

Please know praying this prayer isn't a requirement for the Lord to heal you. His love for you is not conditional. The stories in this book will illustrate to you just how far and wide and deep His love is. He, above all, desires a relationship with you!

LET'S PRAY

"Lord God, I have hope that You are real, and You are able to heal me. Build my faith and show me it is safe to trust You. Calm my soul and help me sense You are near to me.

I choose today—not walking my own walk and depending upon myself—but submitting my life to You and Your astounding love for me. I choose You! I do believe Jesus is Your Son, and I look forward to learning more about Your Holy Spirit, who promises to guide and comfort me. Forgive me of my sins and give me a fresh start. I give my life to You today. In Jesus' Name I pray. Amen."

For more information about Jesus, see the Addendum: The Ultimate Heartbreak.

LET'S ASK

What did I learn today about who God is?

_____

_____

_____

_____

What changes did I make in my relationship with Him?

_____

_____

_____

_____

_____

LET'S DO

If I submitted my life to God today, I'll remember by writing the date down here. It marks a new beginning!

_____

CHAPTER 6

MIRACLE MOMENTS

THERE SHE STOOD—a different hair stylist waiting for me with her comb and scissors. Things had changed. She had changed.

She knew I was writing a book, and at the previous appointment asked about it. Two minutes into my explanation, her voice tensed. Tears filled her eyes. "That's very sad," she said. "Everyone has things happen to them that cause pain and heartbreak."

"Precisely!" I replied. "That's why I'm writing about it. Because God loves us so much, He is ready to heal all of the pain from those memories. When He does heal, the results are amazing!"

Her emotional reaction revealed her own pain. Although she did not share the specific memories she struggled with, God knew them, and before I left, we stood alone together in the early evening shadows, lifting our hearts in prayer. In moments, God lovingly reached down from heaven, extracted her pain, and filled her heart with peace. A great heaviness lifted.

"He reached down from on high and took hold of me;
he drew me out of deep waters."

— Psalm 18:16 NIV

Encouraging her to continue to pray the same way each time another memory of heartache came to mind, I assured her God would always be near, and He would answer.

How she glowed this day! Excitedly, she reported she'd been praying ever since I left last time: "In my car, eating lunch, mixing hair color, wherever I am when something painful comes to mind, I place my hand over my heart and pray—even though it may seem weird if people are around. I feel like a big load has been lifted from my shoulders!"

What a great report! At each appointment, she shares more wonderful stories of the Lord's work in her life.

Jesus promises:

> "Come to me, all you who are weary and burdened,
> and I will give you rest."
>
> **— Matthew 11:28 NIV**

Possibly, the Lord has begun speaking to you about certain memories that triggered raw emotions. You've been reading through page by page in anticipation of discovering this prayer with the promised miracle moments. We're almost there.

He is Able

Remember, no matter what we've experienced or what we've done, God is ready and able to heal us. Numerous times in the New Testament, the word *dunamis* appears in original Greek versions. Generally, *dunamis* refers to "strength, power, or ability." It is the root word of our English words *dynamite, dynamo,* and *dynamic*; however, *dunamis* is not just any power; the word often refers to miraculous power or marvelous works. When we ask Him to heal our hearts, The Lord uses His inherent miraculous power to answer our request!

> "Oh, Lord GOD, you made the skies and the earth with your
> very great power.
> There is nothing too hard for you to do."
>
> **— Jeremiah 32:17 NCV**

The Prayer

Matters of the heart can be very complex, but our prayers need not be complicated for God to respond magnificently.

Prayer, "Pouring our hearts out to God," means we don't have to use big words or long sentences. Imagine picking up a holy cell-phone and talking to One who loves us dearly. The Most High God—the Holy One who loves us without condition—waits to hear from us.

> "Yet the Lord longs to be gracious to you;
> therefore he will rise up to show you compassion.
> For the Lord is a God of justice.
> Blessed are all who wait for him!"
>
> **— Isaiah 30:18 NIV**

Matters of the heart can be very complex, but our prayers need not be complicated for God to respond magnificently.

After attending various training events on prayer for emotional healing, everything changed in my life and resulted in the ministry I'm involved in now. Through the years, personal prayers with friends and family members increased as, together, we asked the Lord to heal specific painful memories. We recognized the remarkable value of prayer at the moment the hurtful memories came to mind. Whether we asked God to reveal a point of pain because we were troubled, or we already clearly identified the damaging memory,

God was ready to gently heal our hearts and replace peace
for our pain.[4]

> ## We recognized the remarkable value of prayer at the moment the hurtful memories came to mind.

* * *

I'm one of those people who isn't very good about doing
something unless I understand why it's important. Because
many others feel the same way, let's break down the parts of
this prayer for heart healing for more complete understanding.
You'll see the prayer outlined below in three different ways:

- A list of the seven steps with detailed explanations
- A list of the seven steps with examples of words
  to say
- A list of the seven steps in simple summary format

One more thing: God's response isn't dependent upon
your confidence. You're here because your hope is ignit-
ing your faith. He will show you He can be trusted. Don't
underestimate God's abilities. He is amazing!

1. Ask God to reveal the memory He plans to heal.

Usually, a hurtful memory has already come to mind. If
not, ask God what memory He wants to heal. There are also
times when you feel troubled or emotional and don't know
why. When that happens, ask the Lord *if* there is a memory

He wants to heal that is connected to these feelings. It may be helpful to look at your notes from earlier chapters.

Often, God heals only one memory at a time. Sometimes, He determines you are ready to be healed of a collection of memories, but you'll sense that at the time you pray. When God heals even one small memory, remember, that healing may bring big results.

If you feel especially emotional, remember tears can be a good thing. Studies show emotional tears contain stress hormones, so tears alone would make you feel better.[5] Add the permanent heart healing of Jesus, and your experience will be astounding!

If you don't feel emotional, don't be concerned, but please know it is safe to allow Jesus into your place of pain. You only need to be willing to open a small window to your heart. The gentle breeze of His magnificent healing will come in.

> *Often, God heals only one memory at a time. Sometimes, He determines you are ready to be healed of a collection of memories, but you'll sense that at the time you pray. When God heals even one small memory, remember, that healing may bring big results.*

2. Place your hand over your heart.

Why place our hands over our hearts? We want to bring focus to our chest area, where we usually feel heartache most intensely. Remember how our brains send signals to our adrenal glands when we experience anxiety, then, our adrenals send stress hormones to our hearts.

Many will tell you, when they place their hands over their hearts to pray, they sense a connection between their physical, emotional, and spiritual selves and God. Nevertheless, if you cannot place your hand over your heart at the time you pray, your prayers will still be answered!

3. Invite the Lord to heal your heart.

Jesus is gentle. He waits for us to ask Him to help us. Do you have hope you will be healed? Now is the time to let down your guard enough to allow the healing touch of One who understands heartbreak. It's important to note you can tell Him how you feel about this memory, even if your words are filled with anguish or despair. He already knows, but your words help you open your heart.

> "Hear, O LORD, *when* I cry with my voice!
> Have mercy also upon me, and answer me.
> *When You said,* 'Seek My face,'
> My heart said to You, 'Your face, LORD, I will seek.'"
>
> **— Psalm 27: 7-8 NKJV**

Have you had so much trauma and stress in life, you've worked hard to build a wall of protection around your heart so you'll never be hurt again? Many of us have done this to avoid being vulnerable or emotionally available to anyone again. Those same walls, though, prevent meaningful relationships with those who truly care about us and love us. That barrier also keeps God out. Will you take a moment to allow Him in, even if you only slightly crack the gate to the protective wall?

4. Ask Him to heal the pain connected to the memory.

Will the pain really go away? Again, here's what God's Word says about that:

> "He heals the brokenhearted
> And binds up their wounds [healing their pain and
> comforting their sorrow]."
>
> **— Psalm 147:3 AMP**

He does not always take the memory away, because memories may be used for good. They influence who we become and are now part of our character; however, the Lord will remove the pain from that memory—the part that clutches at your soul, misshapes your thoughts, and may be keeping you from your destiny. You may be surprised how your thoughts and reasoning change once your heart is healed from wounds in the past. You will no longer be hobbled, and you will have peace in pockets of your heart where peace never existed before.

Some of you may think you have too many scars in your history for God to ever do a complete work. Nothing is impossible for Him. Perhaps you are reading this book because it's time for you to know your heart can be thoroughly healed. Complete healing of every painful memory may happen over time, but He will answer you each time you pray. Your pain will be replaced by His peace.

He will answer you each time you pray.
Your pain will be replaced by His peace.

5. Ask Him to heal any related illness in your mind or body and restore you to good health.

As we read in Chapter 4, there is a close connection between stress and heartache and our physical and mental well-being. In this step, you will ask the Lord to cancel any emotional or physical illness related to the traumatic memory (or memories) you are praying about. The pain from the memory will be healed immediately. Sometimes, your physical health and well-being are restored over time. However God chooses to do this, He will see that the healing work is done.

> "This is what the LORD, the God of your father David, says:
> I have heard your prayer and seen your tears;
> I will heal you."
>
> **— 2 Kings 20:5 NIV**

6. Thank God for your healing.

This is about God and gratefulness. When we express our appreciation to Him, we honor Him for what He has done for us. Have you ever given a gift to someone and they never said, "Thank you?" You may have enjoyed giving it because of your feelings for the recipient. Nevertheless, it would be wonderful to hear them express appreciation for what you did. Their gratitude makes you even more excited about giving gifts to them in the future. Then, magnify the size of the miraculous healing your Creator just provided. How much more should we be motivated to thank Him!

> "I will praise you, Lord, with all my heart.
> I will tell all the miracles you have done."
>
> **— Psalm 9:1 NCV**

7. Breathe again.

You'll probably feel compelled to take a deep breath or two after you pray. That's because as God stunningly brings healing to your heart, you may notice you're holding your breath. Perhaps you unknowingly hit a "pause" button so you didn't miss the incredible sense of Jesus moving through your soul. It's as though life stands still during each miracle moment.

When we breathe deeply at the end of these prayers, I believe the rush of oxygen through our bloodstreams awakens the cells in our bodies to Jesus' healing touch. These deep breaths cause us to feel refreshed, bring closure to our prayer time, and even result in a change in countenance; we experience peace, joy, a knowing—knowing without words that our tomorrows will be different from our yesterdays.

Take your own deep breath. Embrace the incredible realization the Creator of the Universe just touched you in a phenomenal way and destroyed barriers from your past.

"Then the LORD God formed a man from the dust of the ground and breathed into his nostrils the breath of life, and the man became a living being."

— Genesis 2:7 NIV

***

Following is a chart that breaks down each step of prayer with examples. Please keep in mind as you pour your heart out to God, you will probably change your words to fit your circumstances. These examples are simply starting points for you. Again, please know when you speak to God, you are free to make your words your own. Just do your best to cover the key points. God will do the rest.

"Then they cried out to the Lord in their trouble, and he delivered them from their distress."

— Psalm 107:6 NIV

Our relationships with God change with prayer that comes from deep within us. We no longer see Him as a distant God sitting on a throne in the heavens. We feel a divine connection with Him that is very personal.

Examining these simple words, know each word spoken is taken seriously by the Lord. He examines our hearts and knows what we are feeling. His character is genuine and His love is very real. He is able to heal and He is ready.

Seven Steps	You Could Say . . .
1. Ask God to reveal the memory He plans to heal.	*"Thank you, Lord, for bringing the memory to mind that You want to heal today."* **OR** *"Lord, reveal to me the painful memory You plan to heal.* **OR** *"Lord, I feel troubled, and I don't know why. Please reveal what You want to heal in my heart today."*
2. Place your hand over your heart.	*"Lord, I place my hand over my heart."*
3. Invite the Lord into your heart.	*"Lord, I open my heart to Your healing."* **OR** *"Lord, it's hard for me to open my heart to You because of pain from my past. Please help me let You in."*

4. Ask Him to heal the pain connected to the memory.	*"Lord, please heal the pain in my heart connected to this memory."*
5. Ask Him to heal any related illness in your mind or body and restore you to good health.	*"Please heal any emotional or physical illness related to this memory and restore my mind and body to good health."* **OR** *"Lord, please heal all of me . . . mind, body, soul, and spirit.*
6. Thank God for your healing.	*"Thank you, Lord, for the healing You have given me today. You are mighty. You are loving. You are amazing!"*
7. Breathe again.	

As you pour your heart out to God, you will probably change your words to fit your circumstances.

Don't overthink this process, or try reasoning it in your mind. Your healing is God's opportunity to shine. The results are not dependent upon your ability to understand how He's doing it. You only need to trust enough to ask Him. His gentle healing is very real. Talk to Him. He's listening.

To Summarize:

Prayer in Seven Simple Steps

1. Ask God to reveal the memory He plans to heal.

2. Place your hand over your heart.

3. Invite the Lord into your heart.

4. Ask Him to heal the pain connected to the memory (memories).

5. Ask Him to heal any related illness in your mind or body and restore you to good health.

6. Thank God for your healing.

7. Breathe again!

Turn to the back of the book for a
Prayer in Seven Simple Steps bookmark.

The prayer is simple, but His response is profound.

That's it! The prayer is simple, but His response is profound. You may feel immediate relief. You may not feel anything, but God is still responding. Often, people will wake the next morning and do a mental search for the familiar ache in their hearts, only to discover it's gone. If you've successfully hidden those memories from yourself for years, you may not even realize the agony from them has disappeared, but you'll begin to notice a change in your thoughts, behavior, and/or health.

Cameron's Story

Cameron's routine tonsillectomy took a dangerous turn her first night home. Severe hemorrhaging resulted in blood loss and a downward spiral into unconsciousness. Her anxious parents rose as the doctor approached them in the emergency room.

"The artery to her tongue was severed during surgery," the doctor reported, avoiding the look in their eyes. "The repair process is complicated, and the prognosis is not good. I'm sorry to tell you the next time you see her, she will be on a ventilator and on life support."

Miraculously, Cameron surprised everyone by being alert. Unable to talk, she wrote on a tablet, "I love Jesus." Later, "I am a child of God." These words were not previously common to her. In her crisis, she was aware of God's presence in her life. Her next tablet words were, "Please pray!" And they did.

Cameron's quick recovery was miraculous! Unbelievably, she was out of the hospital and at work in a matter of a few weeks. Although her physical improvement was incredible, the trauma from the near-death experience left her emotionally fragile. She cried hard and often. Doctors soon diagnosed PTSD.

Then, she heard about the prayer for heart healing. She didn't see the seven written steps she needed to follow. She heard the instructions and prayed the best way she could remember. Alone, with her hand over her heart, she asked the Lord for help. God answered. God healed.

"My first prayer for heart healing worked immediately. I can't find the words to explain the amazing difference it made. Now, every time another memory from that experience comes to mind, my hand automatically goes to my chest, ready for me to pray. God heals me every time!"

The seven steps provided are meant to be a guideline. Don't be concerned about perfection in the process. Earnestly seek Him in your painful moments and know that God is GOD.

***

Memory by memory, God heals and helps us align our lives toward peace and a brighter future.

As the Author of all Creation tenderly eliminates the pain from our experiences, He sometimes removes the memory altogether. Usually, He allows the memory to stay because it defines our history, shapes our character, and strengthens our faith. The pain from our past no longer has the power to do us harm or keep us hobbled. Memory by memory, God heals and helps us align our lives toward peace and a brighter future. Why? Because He loves us, He promises to heal in His Word, and He desires a relationship with us.

"The LORD said to me, 'You have seen correctly, for I am watching to see that my word is fulfilled.'"

— Jeremiah 1:12 NIV

* * *

The intensity of our struggles does not go unnoticed by God. If you feel too overwhelmed or anxious about this moment of prayer, set it aside. You can still place your hand on your heart and ask God to calm you. Let Him know that you would like for Him to help you be ready for the healing He plans for you. When you do this, you may gather peace from taking a deep breath and relaxing. It may be that ten minutes later, you'll sense you are ready to pray; or perhaps in the middle of the night, you'll awaken and recognize the moment to go ahead and pray for the healing of the memory. The timing is unimportant, but the right time will come because you asked your Creator, the Author of all Mankind, to help you, and He will.

There are more answers. In another chapter, we'll talk about those who struggle with memories that require a few extra steps of prayer. Please be assured God will not let you down and His plans for you are for restoration and peace.

Captured Moments

Prayer is powerful and we can under-utilize it unknowingly. How often do we say things like, "Please pray for me" or "I'll be sure to pray about that"? These are valuable expressions of the need for God to move in our lives, but the miracle moments I refer to here are captured at the time the painful thoughts surface. At the moment we remember something hurtful, we may think our emotions will explode, and we may try to cram the pain back into a place where it can be ignored. Instead, when we immediately pray through the simple prayer steps, we can experience miracle moments—wherever we are, whatever we are doing. (Just like my hairstylist!) By the end of each prayer, we thank Him, take a deep breath or two, and the pain will be gone.

> **At the moment we remember something hurtful, we immediately pray through the simple prayer steps and experience miracle moments.**

If we begin to feel emotional again, we are possibly thinking of a *related* memory. We simply repeat the quick healing prayer. God will heal that wound as well.

A Family Member's Story

While writing this chapter, I suddenly recalled a traumatic time in the life of one of my children. This set of memories, stashed away many years, instantly came alive again as I remembered the words of the doctors, the look on my teenager's face, and the devastation I disguised as concern.

With the resurrected memories, my heart filled with tremendous pressure, and the emotions I had carefully hidden away for so long started to explode. Impulsively, I placed my hand over my heart and prayed the simple heart-healing prayer. Within moments, I was smiling and calm.

God knows what we can handle and when. This particular time of healing for me included a collection of memories about my teenager's illness. God will let me know when it's time for another miracle moment with Him, but these moments occur less frequently as God has been walking me through one hidden heartache after another. My "Brave and Strong" closet is steadily depleting, and God is replacing all of the pain with peace.

Shopping Mall Disclaimer

A friend, after experiencing her own heart healing, became so excited that she began praying for everyone she encountered. Her bold prayers included random people in line at retail stores. Although her intentions were courageous and commendable, she stumbled upon problems along the way:

- Those not wanting this prayer became angry.
- Some may have appreciated the prayer, but it was not the Lord's appointed time for them to receive it.
- Praying boldly, without waiting for prompting from the Holy Spirit, she exposed herself to unsafe situations—both physically and spiritually.

"But wait!" you ask. "Don't you suggest we spread the word about the healing God has for us?" Certainly! Here's the catch: There's a difference between telling people about what our Lord does for us and actually praying for others without submitting first to guidance from God.

Remember the simple steps in praying for heart healing. These steps encourage and engage the person praying in the process. They must be ready and willing to participate, knowing for themselves it's the right time. Once we pray for our healing and comfortably understand the simple steps, there will be opportunities to pray for others. Just as we earlier envisioned all the hurting hearts in a crowded place, there is no shortage of people seeking answers. Wait until you recognize God's tapping on the shoulder urging, "Now!"

"There is a time for everything,
and a season for every activity under the heavens:

a time to be born and a time to die,
a time to plant and a time to uproot,
a time to kill and a time to heal."

— Ecclesiastes 3:1-4 NIV

Returning from a one-day prayer event, I recalled a young woman who traveled a long distance to receive personal prayer. Deeply troubled by her painful past, she explained she could not get beyond the memories. It soon became clear that it was time for her miracle moment. As we prayed, the touch of Jesus to her heart was so dramatic she hardly knew how to respond, crying one moment and laughing the next. As the Lord continued healing her heart, peace swept over her face. She couldn't stop smiling as she returned to her seat. Only God could do this!

Let's notice: 1) she asked for prayer, 2) she was engaged in the process, and 3) it was clear the Holy Spirit was saying, "Now!"

For Those in Occupations Facing Frequent Trauma

Although the prayer steps outlined in this chapter apply to everyone, prayers may be tailored to meet specific circumstances. Certain active-duty military personnel, first responders, and others dealing with vicarious trauma may face heartrending crises daily. When each tragic moment occurs, no matter where we pray, God hears our words and He responds.

Remember Tom, the military and police veteran who told us first responders would not talk about their traumatic experiences because any signs of mental or emotional weakness could result in the loss of their jobs. Tom and I talked about praying for heart healing after each traumatic moment. Tom replied, "When I was a cop, I could have sat in my patrol car and prayed at any time, and I wouldn't have had to worry about anyone else knowing."

The Lord God hears us, and He will respond! In a sense, He is our own personal First Responder, always ready and waiting for our call to Him.

For first responders or others at risk for sudden, major trauma, God reacts immediately to our prayers—whether in patrol cars, in war zones, or burn centers—anywhere, God is there. Must we pray aloud? No. The Lord hears our prayers whether spoken aloud or not. Must we place our hands over our heart if we feel self-conscious? No.

The Lord God hears us, and He will respond! In a sense, He is our own personal First Responder, always ready and waiting for our call to Him.

Here's an example of the simple prayer tailored for your circumstances:

Prayer in Seven Simple Steps for First Responders

1. Speak to God about your pain from the traumatic event.

2. Place your hand over your heart.

3. Invite the Lord into your heart.

4. Ask Him to heal the pain connected to the event.

5. Ask Him to heal any related illness in your mind or body and restore you to good health.

6. Thank God for your healing.

7. Breathe again!

What about the multitude of other difficult or tragic memories we've crammed away over the years? The Lord will bring each one to mind at the right time, in the right way, for His healing. The next few chapters teach us more about ongoing and deeper healing.

Let's consider a valuable extra step that is especially helpful to release anxiety for those exposed to the frequent tragedy of others. Figuratively, let's place the burdens we've been carrying for others in our cupped hands in front of us. Describing the pain and heaviness of these burdens to God, we lift our burden-holding hands, open our fingers, and release them to Him. Now His, they are no longer ours to carry.

> "I removed the burden from their shoulders;
> their hands were set free from the basket.
> In your distress you called and I rescued you."
>
> **— Psalm 81:6-7 NIV**

Our prayers do not have to be complicated for God to respond magnificently. When thoughts of a difficult event come to our minds, will we pack the memory back away in our hearts or will we pray for healing? Pack it away or pray it away? It's our choice.

When thoughts of a difficult event come to our minds, will we pack the memory back away in our hearts or will we pray for healing?

A Prayer of Commitment and Protection for Those Exposed to Vicarious Trauma

Often, Christians pray a prayer for protection and spiritual strength taken from the verses found in Ephesians 6:10–17. These verses focus on how we can cloak ourselves in God's armor, much as a medieval knight would have protected himself with his physical armor.

Below is a similar prayer for those who regularly experience vicarious trauma. It can be prayed to establish a strong foundation of protection around you, but during each day, quick heart-healing prayers may be prayed at moments of crisis.

"Heavenly Father, thank you for the occupation you have given me. I submit it to You and ask that I may honor You as I participate in this calling. Please remind me I can pray in the moment to guard my heart against any traumatic effects of my work.

I choose to put on Your armor of protection. I will stand for truth, and I'll do my best to honor You with the way I live my life. Help me to know the things You say in Your Word and give me strength to live by them. I trust You in faith and am grateful You have shown me the way to eternal life.

Thank You, Lord, for your response to this prayer. I also thank You for the healing that will come to my heart from past wounds. Lord God, You are Mighty, and I receive the healing You have for me no matter the depth of the wounds. You are able and faithful.

While You are protecting me, please enable me to show love and compassion in all I do. May lives be changed because of the calling You've given me to help others.

In Jesus' name I pray. Amen."

LET'S ASK

As we pray, believe in the Lord's amazing work in our hearts. When we come to Him with hope, He provides peace for our pain.

The Lord healed these painful personal memories today:

_____

_____

_____

_____

_____

_____

_____

Today I prayed for healing from the following vicarious trauma I felt for others:

_____

_____

_____

_____

_____

_____

CHAPTER 7

TIMED RELEASE

MY HANDS WERE SHAKING as I hung up the phone. I'd just received the news we would be addressing the topic of trauma at an upcoming ministry event. I attended many previous conferences like this and always had an extraordinary experience with God. But this was different.

No one knew I still had hidden pain.

Once I heard the word "trauma," I knew their prayers with me about trauma would result in a meltdown of legendary proportions. For over seventeen years, one tragedy after another followed my life: divorce, diseases, deaths, losses, failures—crisis after crisis continuously coming like an avalanche. I stuffed all the heartbreak into my "Brave and Strong" closet and put on a smile. If God chose to unlock all of that well-disguised pain during that event, it was going to be messy.

For weeks, I battled anxiety over the anticipated scene and I lived on the verge of panic attacks. When the dreaded day came, something surprising happened.

While at the event, other duties distracted me during the time dedicated to praying for trauma. What a relief. No meltdown. No embarrassment. No scene. I contentedly kept my anxieties crammed down in my heart to deal with some other day.

Exhausted entering my hotel room that evening, I fell across the bed. Suddenly, a quiet gentle voice whispered, "Now." A flood of tortuous memories raced through my mind, an explosive feeling arose in my chest, and I cried—and cried—and cried. It seemed every tear, filled with a measure of grief, called out to Jesus. I sensed warm healing through my body. When the crying finally ended, I felt washed with calm.

The Lord healed many traumatic memories that night in His timed-release manner designed just for me. In the months and years to come, the healing journey continued.

Bit by bit, He emptied my "Brave and Strong" closet from the collected years of pain. Whether one painful memory or a whole series of memories, God provided healing at exactly the right time. Often, even in unexpected places, a difficult memory came into my head. Stopping to pray, the Lord released me from the gripping fingers of anxiety.

* * *

When we hear the term "timed release," we often think of medications designed to release a steady stream of drug in our bodies over a set period. They relieve physical symptoms of disease or pain. Similarly, God's timed-release healing comes periodically over time to relieve the effects of heartache on our bodies, minds, and spirits.

The best news: God's timed-release healing, done on His clock and His calendar, produces permanent results, not temporary control as medications do.

Our first courageous step is to release to God more painful memories from our past. Over time, that closet full of pain empties, and we experience more and more peace.

"Cast all your anxiety on Him because He cares for you."

— 1 Peter 5:7 NIV

Relying on our own bravery and strength (self-dependence) exhausts us and drains us of joy. Trusting God for our bravery and strength (God-dependence) energizes and encourages us, filling us with joy. With courage fueled by Him, we rise each morning, with our souls and spirits increasingly rested and refreshed.

> *Relying on our own bravery and strength (self-dependence) exhausts us and drains us of joy. Trusting God for our bravery and strength (God-dependence) energizes and encourages us, filling us with joy.*

"But as for me, I will sing about your power.
Each morning I will sing with joy about your unfailing love.
For you have been my refuge, a place of safety when I am in distress."

— Psalm 59:16 NLT

My Hairstylist

Remember my hairstylist who prayed whenever a painful memory came to mind: while driving her car, mixing hair color or eating lunch. She recently updated me, "I used to relive painful incidents from my past over and over again in my mind, even though I'd try to train my mind not to think about them anymore. Wherever I looked for help before, nothing changed in here (as she pointed to her heart). This new way to pray helps me get up every morning and get out the door. It's changed my life."

One memory at a time and one prayer at a time, she continues to turn to God and He is healing her heart. In His timed-release manner, He is changing her life!

> "Evening, morning and noon I cry out in distress,
> and He hears my voice."

— Psalm 55:17 NIV

Melanie's Story

Her father's abusive behavior and her mother's passivity were traits Melanie embraced as she became an adult. After dating an abusive young man for two years, she was left with her heart broken and wounds so deep she wasn't sure she'd ever heal.

> *"It especially hurt because I fell so deeply in love with him before he broke up with me. In the end, the relationship left me with nothing but pain. I'd pray, and I believed God would work everything out, but I had no idea how He'd do it.*
>
> *"Then I heard you explain how to pray for heart healing. After that, each time I would think of another painful moment from that relationship, I would pray the heart-healing prayer and I began to feel better and better. Now, that damaging relationship doesn't affect me at all!*
>
> *"Oh, and since then, I've met a man who has been absolutely wonderful for me. We share the same*

belief in God and he encourages me in ways I'd always only hoped for. I believe every time I prayed for healing from that past relationship I came one step closer to being ready for this healthy new friendship!"

Over time, God rescued Melanie from her past and prepared her for her future.

Types of Memories

Two categories of memory are short-term and long-term, based on how long we store the memory.[6] Short-term memory is kept in mind for a short time until we dismiss it or transfer it to long-term memory. Long-term memory is our brain's system for storing, managing, and retrieving information.

Sometimes we repress long-term memories. This means we unconsciously block the memories because they are associated with a high level of stress or trauma. These repressed memories are basically hiding from our conscious minds, but God knows exactly where they are.

At the Laundromat

Moving to the Los Angeles area from Texas, my husband and I experienced many life changes. Gone was the sprawling home with the convenient laundry room next to our kitchen.

Each time I loaded the laundry into my SUV, I struggled with anxiety. It seemed useless to sit in our chair to rally energy before I left. Carting the laundry bags into the laundromat, I'd march myself through thankful thoughts during my time there, and I hustled to finish quickly. In spite of these efforts, I always returned home needing to rest and decompress from the stressful experience.

One day, my brother questioned why it was such a big deal for me to go to the laundromat. He traveled for work, went to nearby laundromats, dumped the clothes in to wash and dry, and returned to his hotel. Plain and simple.

I offered a quick reply about all the change we experienced, and how I felt unsettled in our neighborhood; nevertheless, his words rattled in my head for days. The next week, I returned to the laundromat and things changed.

I eased myself out of my house and drove to the laundromat. Staring at the entry doors, I seemed stuck to the seat, with fingers frozen on the steering wheel and anxiety building inside. Finally I grasped the need to turn to Father God for help.

"Oh, Lord, why do I struggle with this? Why can't going to the laundromat be just a matter-of-fact part of my weekly routine?" His answer was swift.

I immediately thought of myself at twenty-one with two tiny girls, living in a second-level apartment in a massive complex. Twice each week, I carried the girls and all the dirty laundry downstairs to a nearby laundromat. Although I hated that chore and the inconvenience of it, I hated my life even more. It was filled with deep heartbreak that wove like poison through my soul.

God traveled to a remote file in my "Brave and Strong" heart closet to find these decades-old memories, but once the memories were exposed, my emotions felt raw. I knew it was time to face it head-on and deal with that deeply buried repressed pain.

With my hand on my chest, I prayed, "Lord, please come to my heart and heal the place where this pain is stored. Please heal me of any related infirmity, too. Thank You for my healing. In Jesus' name. Amen."

That's all I said, yet I took a deep breath and experienced another miracle moment.

I finished the prayer, grabbed the car keys, washed, dried, and folded the laundry, returned to the house, and started cooking dinner before I realized what had happened. God revealed to me this source of pain, answered my prayer for heart healing, and readjusted my perspective on the entire laundromat experience! No more anxiety. No more meditating on thankful thoughts. I returned home in a blur of energy not needing to pause and decompress.

Since then, although I still don't exactly delight in this chore, I'm now free of any ancient, anxious memories or stress. Am I grateful! Does Almighty God care about my difficulties getting my wash done every week? Absolutely!

✳✳✳

Biography Bookmarks

Imagine with me that each of us has a biography of our lives on a table in front of us. The pages include stories of fun celebrations, memorable gatherings, and special birthdays, but there are bookmarks at pages documenting each of our painful experiences or memories. Although some of us may have many bookmarks in our biographies, others will have few. Each bookmarked page represents one moment of heartache. "My Mother Died of Lung Disease" would be an entire chapter of my biography, but the bookmarked pages each speak of one piercing memory that continued to tug at my heart.

- When the doctor delivered the news Mother had a spot on her lung, a bookmarked page was added to my biography.

- When her lung collapsed during the biopsy and she almost died, a bookmark was added to another page of my biography.

- When the burns from her cancer radiation treatments were so bad she needed readmission to the hospital, another bookmarked page was added.

- As we eventually placed the last of the pink roses on her casket, a bookmarked page was added.

The Lord took me to each bookmarked page one at a time, rather than healing me of all the related memories at once.

When just the right time comes for canceling the effects of a heartbreak, God shows us. A tormenting thought of abuse . . . A horrible visual experience years ago . . . A hurtful, festering insult . . . A heartbreaking loss . . . Betrayal by someone once trusted . . . The Lord sees these biography bookmarks of pain and heartache and desires for our hearts to be healed—in His time, in His way.

Sometimes our emotions feel raw because we allowed that moment from our past to escape our hidden closets of pain. As we review those bookmarked pages with the Lord, we are free to speak to Him about how we feel. We may hear ourselves say, "God, this HURTS!" or "God, I'm so ANGRY!" or "God, please HELP!" Sometimes, we need to add, "God, please FORGIVE me!"

He's listening. He loves us. He's ready to make it all better. Pray through this again:

Prayer in Seven Simple Steps

(Use your own words as you pour your heart out to God.)

1. Ask God to reveal the memory He plans to heal (if you don't already know it).

2. Place your hand over your heart.

3. Invite the Lord into your heart.

4. Ask Him to heal the pain connected to the memory (memories).

5. Ask Him to heal any related illness in your mind or body.

6. Thank God for your healing.

7. Breathe again!

Let's imagine now that we're standing with God, reviewing our bookmarked biography pages, and He, Our Creator, deletes the pain-filled parts that document terrible memories. It's not that our pain wasn't real or wasn't horrible.

It's His power, and even His joy as your Creator to wipe out the pain and hurt. Our bookmarked page may remain with a record of the event, but the documented wounds cannot hold us back. We are no longer hobbled by the agony of heartbreaking moments. God's peace replaces our pain.

We only need to trust God enough to open our hearts and let Him in.

At times, God deletes several bookmarked moments at once. Like a collage or slideshow, the hurting memories may flash through our minds at once, while God wipes away every torturous thought. Healing tears flow. Whew. Hand over the heart. Deep breath. Deep breath. Deep breath. Visions and visions from bookmarked pages disappear and calm replaces the effects of their trauma.

We only need to trust God enough to open our hearts and let Him in.

Once we trust God with an open heart, we may find whether we're driving down the road, reading a book, talking on the phone, or busy at work, suddenly it's there—that stabbing memory from our past that we thought we'd successfully hidden deep in the closet marked "Brave and Strong."

No matter where we are or what we're doing, when God brings a painful memory to mind, it's for a reason. His desire is to reach deeply into our souls to extract and deal with the very source of ongoing heartache and stress. When it's His timing to heal it, be ready to release it!

Timed-Release and Physical Healing

Just as emotional healing may be done in a timed-release manner, so may the physical healing related to it. Those "repairs" may involve a long process.

I would awake and smother stressful concerns of the new day with thoughts of the meals I would prepare. Thoughts of food were my coping mechanism, and eating food was my antidepressant.

Over the years, as my clothing size increased, so did my anxiety about how I looked and felt. I began to search for answers beyond my own will power. I went to counseling. I prayed for myself, had others pray for me, went through different approaches to prayer, read books, watched videos, and pounded on God's door for help.

Finally, a huge breakthrough occurred when friends prayed with me for the healing of the sad memories and deep emotional ties to my father's battle with cancer and his ultimate death. The morning after that prayer, I awoke feeling strangely calm. As I waited, expecting the familiar obsessive thoughts about food, they never came!

My heartache related to Dad had fueled the compulsion to eat. Prayer for heart healing led to normal thoughts of food; sometimes, I even forgot to eat until my rumbling stomach reminded me!

Those of us who abuse substances like food, drugs, sex, or shopping are rarely able to permanently stop these activities without help from the Almighty. His solution is not just a matter of making up our minds and strengthening our will to change. When the Lord points out the source of our pain and erases its torment, incredibly, our compulsions ease.

Our Lord created us with an intricately interwoven body, mind, and spirit. The ripple effect of heartache through our beings is complex. In some cases, like mine, the physical healing from the influence of heartache takes place in a timed-release manner. The damage we do through self-medicating may require changes in lifestyle or habits. Perhaps we need to learn more about caring for our health and wellness in new ways.

For example, I've since learned how my body responded to the chronic stress I experienced for so many years, producing additional glucose (sugar) into my bloodstream to provide the energy needed to persevere. That works great when faced with short-term shocking events, but continued chronic stress kept the glucose flowing into my system far more than it was ever needed.[7]

I added to the problem by choosing comfort food such as cookies over apples. To explain in simple terms, my digestive system and immune system suffered, and my body became insulin resistant. This knowledge solved a personal mystery as to why, once I tried to lose weight, my success was limited. I'm traveling toward improved health and wellness, but there are more things to learn and habits to change before it becomes a permanent lifestyle.

I'm so grateful for this new understanding.

Cardio Compactors

Very few of us know how to effectively deal with awful things that happen in our lives. Instead, we cope by cramming the tormenting thoughts on top of other thoughts inside us.

In her later years, Mom bought a home with an electric trash compactor. Installed into the kitchen cabinets, it stood about half the vertical size of a dishwasher. With the flip of a switch, the machine pressed everything in tighter, making room for more. Sometimes, she would overfill the compactor, and it would begin to malfunction.

When we compact painful thoughts into our hearts to make room for more, we're creating our own *cardio* (heart) *compactors*. In time, all of that cardio compacting can also lead to malfunctioning.

I still remember the doctor's concerned expression as he announced a possible six-month life expectancy for the man who'd raised me, employed me, and gave me my identity.

Treatments weakened him and sickened him. I watched him suffer. Even warm remembrances registered pain inside me—Dad's tender glances when he arrived at the office, sharing precious moments as his body tired, witnessing his courageous acceptance as I listened to him reflect on time lost.

Eventually came discussions of advanced directives, of wills, and carrying on with the family business. Just days after his funeral, we returned to work, attempting some form of normalcy. Brave and strong on the outside, I felt shattered on the inside, and I paid a price. My health gradually declined for years afterward.

Along with the sheer heartbreak of Dad's death, I crammed it all in a place far away. My cardio compactor worked overtime and grief was a constant companion.

Although the pain was much, and deep, I truly experienced that there is nothing impossible for God. His love isn't the kind we experience here on earth, but is a beautiful gift not based on measuring up, working out, looking right, being smart, thinking perfectly, or achieving success.

The more I locked the pain away, the easier it was to avoid it; however, those hidden hurts still impacted my thoughts, my motivations, my actions, and even my courage.

Eventually, through prayer, I came to know that in my coping by compacting, God was ready to work in me in a timed-release manner until all the hurt was eliminated and my heart was healed. Although the pain was much, and deep, I truly experienced that there is nothing impossible for God. His love isn't the kind we experience here on earth, but is a beautiful gift not based on measuring up, working out, looking right, being smart, thinking perfectly, or achieving success. He loved me just as I was. I didn't have to wait until I was a "good person" to turn to Him. The only thing required was to quiet my mind, open my heart, look to Him, and say, "Help!"

Whatever pain we experience in life, our hearts will stay safe when we let them rest with God. We are cherished and loved by Him. May these words reach our innermost beings and touch our hearts with truth.

> "The LORD's love never ends;
> his mercies never stop.
>
> They are new every morning;
> LORD, your loyalty is great."

— Lamentations 3:22-23 NCV

* * *

LET'S PRAY

Heavenly Father, I give my heart to You for healing. I accept even if You, at this time, only want just one memory healed. Over time, I ask you to heal any wound negatively affecting my life. If I've compacted pain deep inside me, I ask You to expose it. Please do this in Your timed-release manner, in a way You know I can handle, and replace the pain with peace.

If my physiology needs healing in a timed-release manner, I pray for patience, wisdom, and understanding. Ultimately, I pray for health and wholeness throughout my body.

With each miracle moment, please build my faith and my understanding of Your acceptance and love for me. In Jesus' Name, I pray. Amen.

LET'S ASK

When have I coped by compacting?

_____

_____

_____

_____

_____

What main heartbreak or set of memories is God is reminding me of that I have hidden from myself?

_____

_____

_____

_____

_____

_____

God did this in response to my prayer:

_____

_____

_____

_____

_____

_____

Here are two or three difficult memories from my biography:

_____

_____

_____

_____

_____

_____

_____

_____

Using the steps provided earlier, and customizing them for my situation, I pray for healing from the pain of these memories.

CHAPTER 8

DEEPER STILL

HANK SHIFTED UNEASILY in his seat in response to the interviewer's questions. A member of the initial entry team during a terrorist shooting, Hank's mission was to locate and isolate the shooter. Hank couldn't stop to help the injured. His eyes connected briefly with those of the victims as he stepped past them. Later, Hank learned many had died. His eyes, clouded with pain as he described the scene, revealed the deep ache and heavy heart he carried. Hailed a hero, his inability to help the wounded caused an incredible struggle within.

"I cannot forget the looks in their eyes, and I am burdened daily by guilt." This courageous man's words provided a window into his troubled soul. He followed protocol and did what was expected. Encouraging words spoken by others, and even his own reasoning, failed to rescue him from the heaviness he feels each day. And, medications? They might suppress the agony, but it would just return another day.

Prayer for heart healing could accomplish much for this hero, but additional prayerful steps might be needed to completely lift the burden of guilt from him.

Sometimes, beyond the heartbreak, we become chained to experiences we just can't get past. The chains seem unbreakable, and we're unable to fully realize God's plans for us. There's good news, though. When we turn to God with our specific prayer, He carries the keys to unlock the chains that keep us bound.

> "He has sent Me to heal the brokenhearted,
> To proclaim liberty to the captives,
> And the opening of the prison to *those who are* bound."
>
> **— Isaiah 61:1 NKJV**

Continued Prayer Required (CPR)

When we've prayed the seven-step prayer, but continue to experience torment related to the same memory, additional prayer may be required. We'll call this Continued Prayer Required (CPR).

The pain in our hearts may be healed, and we sense more peace, but deep inside remains a wrong attitude or negative behavior still attached to the memory. When we can't shake it, we may still be tied to our past.

The continued prayer required may differ from one time to the next. How we pray can be determined by a little detective work on our part. Much like a doctor listens to our hearts with a stethoscope, God examines our hearts with His Holy Spirit.

> "Deal with everyone according to all they do,
> since you know their hearts (for you alone know every human heart)."
>
> **— 1 Kings 8:39 NIV**

Imagine sitting in a heavenly examining room talking with God, the Great Physician. Much like King David did in the Bible, we ask this of God:

> "Create in me a pure heart, God,
> and make my spirit right again."
>
> **— Psalm 51:10 NCV**

We ask Him to purify our hearts, filling us with clean thoughts and right desires related to the heartache. God pulls out His holy stethoscope and says, "Well, let's examine your heart and see if any problems remain that could prevent your complete freedom and release from this memory."

Almost certainly the first place He'll check will be the area of forgiveness.

1. Is there anyone we need to forgive in relation to the memory?

A tough one. Someone or something may have hurt us terribly. We want our offenders to pay. What God knows and we may not, is we're the ones who pay when we don't forgive. When we refuse to forgive, bitterness, resentment, and anger take hold of us and start to enslave us. They nag at our efforts for happiness and rob us of joy. To not forgive is like taking poison ourselves and waiting for our offenders to die.

Jesus gave us beautiful instructions on how to pray to Father God. His words are commonly referred to as "The Lord's Prayer." In a portion of it we read:

> "Forgive us for our sins,
> just as we have forgiven those who sinned against us."
>
> **— Matthew 6:12 NCV**

Oh, how we need to be forgiven for our own sins! With our request to God for this forgiveness, we receive instructions to be ready to forgive those who have hurt us. No matter how difficult this assignment is, the results of our obedience are phenomenal.

Everything inside us may be screaming, "No!" We may feel the impulse to run away. If our pain is still so raw that we cannot consider forgiving, God will help us. He will. At the right time. In the right way. And our lives will change. We need only to be willing for Him to help us.

Forgiving people who caused disaster for us does not excuse what they did or said. Furthermore, forgiving others does not necessarily make it safe or appropriate to re-establish a relationship with them. God will deal with them separately, as He sees fit, but when we forgive them, we are taking a big step to unlock the chains holding us to that painful memory.

A few of us may not have anyone else to forgive; however, if we examine our thoughts, we may realize we still need to forgive *ourselves*. Our own wrong decisions or bad choices can often lead to a lifetime of regret. If we ask Him, God reveals any necessity to forgive ourselves.

We forgive others, we forgive ourselves—and God forgives us!

Forgiving people who caused disaster for us does not excuse what they did or said. Furthermore, forgiving others does not necessarily make it safe or appropriate to re-establish a relationship with them.

***

One New Year's Eve, I listed three things I wanted God to do for me in the coming year. As a young mother, I was shocked at my anger toward my kids. I'm embarrassed to say, I even shoved my daughter across her room during a yelling match one evening. I resented my situation, and I was bitter to be paying a huge price for mistakes I'd made. It was impossible to get those thoughts out of my mind. Desperate for an end to the anger, resentment, and bitterness I felt, I wrote them on the list. After a heartfelt prayer, I slipped the paper between the pages of my Bible.

One day, I had a very disturbing thought. I suddenly knew I needed to forgive the person I felt hurt me the most. That had to be God talking to me, because it sure wasn't my idea! To make matters worse, I realized I needed to ask this person *to forgive me* for the things I'd done, too. No way that was going to happen. I shut all those thoughts down right away. I shut them down again when they awakened me during the night. I shut them down again and again throughout each day—but all without success. Like a balloon in water, no matter how hard I tried to submerge it, the knowledge that I must forgive and ask forgiveness surfaced over and over.

Finally, I drafted a letter, laying out all the words I knew needed to be said. (In this case, a letter was necessary because a personal conversation would not have been emotionally safe for me.) Just writing the draft was painstaking. The related heartache was so intense I'd have to put my pen down and walk away for days. It took three months to finally finish that letter. Adding the address and stamp took more days. Volcanic feelings swelled within me and tears streamed down my face as I finally shuffled to the mailbox. The door to the mailbox squeaked as I opened it. I tossed the envelope in and slammed the door shut.

Suddenly, a huge weight lifted from my shoulders. What an incredible sensation! Since that day, I have not again struggled with that anger, bitterness, or resentment. Why? I asked God for help. Although it took a while, I obeyed His instructions to forgive and to ask forgiveness. I never heard from the person to whom I mailed that letter, but it didn't matter. God responded to my obedience with a sure and permanent healing from that deep, raw heartache.

And the daughter whom I shoved across the room? When I asked her forgiveness, she'd already forgotten it ever happened. Another miracle.

Like trying to push a balloon under water, no matter how hard I tried, the knowledge that I must forgive and ask forgiveness surfaced over and over.

Isn't it wonderful to know God doesn't have to think about it for three months before He forgives us? When we sincerely ask Him to forgive us, He does so immediately. That's His character. What an extraordinary example for us all.

There's just one directive. If we desire the amazing gift of God's forgiveness, we must be ready to pay it forward.

"For if you forgive other people when they sin against you,
your heavenly Father will also forgive you.
But if you do not forgive others their sins,
your Father will not forgive your sins."

— Matthew 6:14-15 NIV

God's ways sometimes surprise us, especially the remarkable change He brings about in us when we choose to honor His instructions and to forgive. He knows what we went through. He knows every tear we've cried and every hidden fury we've felt. He also knows of our struggles to obey Him and forgive others, but the rewards are tremendous!

> **He knows what we went through.**
> **He knows every tear we've cried**
> **and every hidden fury we've felt.**
> **He also knows of our struggles to**
> **obey Him and forgive others,**
> **but the rewards are tremendous!**

***

The Great Physician moves His holy stethoscope to another place over our hearts. The examination continues.

2. Can we give responsibility for our offenders over to God?

It's one thing to forgive what someone has done to us. It's another to let go of wanting them to pay for what they did. When we forgive *and* release our offenders to God, we're disconnecting any further hold they have on us (and we on them).

The Lord, such a righteous, effective, and wise disciplinarian, will handle those who hurt us.

"Do not judge, and you will not be judged.
Do not condemn, and you will not be condemned.
Forgive, and you will be forgiven."

— Luke 6:37 NIV

We imagine God's face glowing with joy over us as we continue to examine our hearts with Him.

3. Did we react to trauma, stress, or heartbreak with wrong attitudes or actions?

"Hurting people hurt people." If our response to painful memories has been hurtful, or if our behavior makes us miserable because we know our behavior is wrong, then we most likely are dealing with sin. What is sin? It's something thought, said, or done that goes against the laws and character of God. From a genuine place inside of us, we express our regret to God. We ask for forgiveness and choose to turn away from sinful behavior. This is often called "repenting."

Is God telling us it's time for change? It's time to stop hurting others and ourselves. It's time to turn away from damaging behavior stemming from our own wounds. Deeply seated sin is harder to break away from, but God, who is compassionate and loves us without conditions, waits for us, ready to help us cut our ties to even the worst behavior.

Amazingly, when we do this, God forgives us, and He removes the record of our ever committing this sin. It's as though it never happened!

> "He has taken our sins away from us
> as far as the east is from west."

— Psalm 103:12 NCV

As soon as we sincerely repent, the lock opens and the chains binding us to our past fall off!

By this time:

1. We've forgiven anyone who needs to be forgiven.

2. We've turned the discipline of any offenders over to God.

3. We've repented of all we've done wrong in response to our wounds.

Now, there's one last step. God completes His examination of us and asks us, "Would you let me remove this from your life now?"

> *God, who is compassionate*
> *and loves us without conditions,*
> *waits for us, ready to help us cut*
> *our ties to even the worst behavior.*

4. Are we ready to give it up?

It's possible some of our pain and behavior became part of our identities. It defined us. It's how people knew us and labeled us. Are we ready to hand it all over to God?

No matter how established the wrong thoughts or actions, God desires to remove them from our lives.

Let's reach inside ourselves, take hold of the final effects of the tormenting, painful memories, and symbolically place them in our cupped hands in front of us. Anger, bitterness, jealousy, frustration, guilt, criticism, shame, resentment, suicide, cutting, and more are all typical issues that cling to us, hoping we won't release them. Lifting our hands to the Lord, we release all of these unwanted thoughts and actions to Him, knowing He will take them away forever. It's up to us to never take them back.

The God of all creation—the One who designed us and loves us without barriers or conditions—is ready to take these tormenting things away from us. This process takes us another step closer to the remarkable destiny He plans for us. How grateful we feel for His abundant and undeserved miracles on our behalf!

> "I will tell about the Lord's kindness
> and praise him for everything he has done."
>
> **— Isaiah 63:7 NCV**

Haley's Story

While Haley was in training as a mentor to other women, she gradually remembered horrifying events from her childhood.

Her loving parents unknowingly left her with babysitters who abused her. The assaults happened with warnings not to tell or "bad things" would happen to her family. Her experiences were so appalling the emotional damage lasted long into her adult life.

Years ago, her young mind stuffed these memories away in a secret place, and when they eventually surfaced, she felt devastated. Her voice strained as she described the memories. I swallowed back my tears listening to her share her pain with me.

Haley's experience impacted more than her heart. Her spirit was crushed, too. Her heart healing became real in a matter of minutes. The stabbing pain was gone, but she admitted an ongoing battle with anger and bitterness. Her abusers had scarred her heart and altered her life.

Situations like this call for extra action, but God is still God, and nothing is too difficult for Him. Continued prayer was required (CPR).

Haley had already forgiven everyone involved, and she had let go of her judgment against her offenders, but anger and bitterness still plagued her. Unable to shake these feelings, through CPR, Haley apologized to God and asked His forgiveness—she repented—realizing the powerful control they had over her thoughts and actions. Placing the anger and the bitterness symbolically in her cupped hands, she raised them up to the King of Kings and the Lord of Lords—the One who would take these sins away from her and who would help her not let them return.

It's important to note that she did not need to repent for being abused. What was done to her was inexcusable and was certainly not her fault.

Haley and I discussed this together; however, please know when you pray, your words can be just between you and God. Most important is to pray the simple seven-step prayer at the moment the painful memory comes to mind (when possible), adding CPR as needed. As you do, your trust in God will continue to build as He demonstrates His love and healing power for you.

Several months later, I asked Haley if she had any updates for me since our prayer time together. "Yes," she said, "I have lost 65 unwanted pounds, and I'm more assertive in almost everything I do in life!"

Most important is to pray the simple seven-step prayer at the moment the painful memory comes to mind (when possible), adding CPR as needed.
As you do, your trust in God will continue to build as He demonstrates His love and healing power for you.

***

We read this verse in Chapter One, but let's take another look at it:

> "The Lord is close to the brokenhearted
> and saves those who are crushed in spirit."
>
> **— Psalm 34:18 NIV**

Early writers of the Bible wrote mostly in Hebrew. The Hebrew word used for "close" (karov) in this verse, means, "close enough to touch." It goes on to mean when He saves the crushed in spirit, He's "making room" to free us from worries and issues that hold us back or cause us stress. He saves us from what oppresses and constricts our inward life.[8]

When our hearts break and we seek God, we won't have to look far, because He is close enough for us to touch Him. Wow! When we feel crushed in spirit—chained to tormenting thoughts and actions—He will heal us and rescue us.

God's love for you is pure, without flaws. If it's hard for you to accept this love, ask Him to heal the memories in your heart that make you feel that way. You now know how to do it. Are wrong thoughts or actions tying you to awful experiences? You can apply a little extra prayer (CPR) and know He is ready to cut the cords that bind you.

When we deal with grief, failure, despair, or anything that robs us of peace and joy; when the effects of Post Traumatic Stress Disorder haunt us; now we know to:

1. Pray the simple seven-step prayer for heart healing.

2. Allow God to continue healing us in His timed-release manner.

3. Go to Him with CPR for persistent issues holding us back.

4. Ask Him to replace peace for our pain.

Whether trapped by our past or tangled in our present, God will reconcile our past and set our sights on the significant future He plans for us. Others can encourage us, guide us, and inspire us, but those are horizontal relationships. The only One with power to permanently remove these issues from our lives is our Creator. When we adjust our hearts from these horizontal relationships to look vertically to Him from our innermost being, He is ready to assist us with His almighty power.[9]

When our hearts break and we seek God, we won't have to look far, because He is close enough for us to touch Him.

***

At times, we may feel so weighed down by the wounds and stresses of life we know we don't want to handle them alone. Perhaps we've forgiven, repented, and released, but we still struggle to unlock our future with peace. We are not alone.

Excellent organizations and reliable resources are available to support us in prayer and teach us more about the extraordinary love and power of God. We don't have to do this by ourselves. An up-to-date list of possible resources may be found at www.CyndyBartelli.com.

***

LET'S ASK

Though my heart was healed in Chapter 6, what related actions or thoughts do I still battle with?

_____

_____

_____

_____

_____

_____

_____

If I haven't already prayed about them, below are steps I plan to take to go deeper in the healing process.

_____

_____

_____

_____

_____

_____

_____

LET'S PRAY

"Thank you, Lord, for healing my heart from the brokenness and despair of my painful memory. I am comforted in the knowledge that You are near as I continue to pray.

There are people connected to this memory who I feel damaged me or made me suffer. I know I need to forgive them. Please help me to do so. I choose now to forgive _____, _____, _____, and myself (if needed). I release responsibility for them over to You. I recognize these people are Your responsibility and not mine.

In spite of this heart healing and Your forgiveness for my sins, I admit I still struggle with the following related feelings, actions, and thoughts:

_____

_____

_____

_____

_____

_____

Please forgive me for these things, because I know they are wrong and they don't honor Your ways or Your instructions.

Lord, I am so sorry I have behaved this way (or thought this way). Now, I take all of these actions and emotions and release them to You. [Symbolically place them in your cupped hands in front of you.] I let go of this behavior, and I ask that you take it away from me forever. Please cancel my connection to these sins. In Jesus' name, I pray. Amen."

CHAPTER 9

PATHWAY TO PEACE

MYLA DOESN'T REMEMBER the first time she saw her father hit her mother. She was small enough to hide under the bed, but there was no way to hide from the sounds of her mother's cries. Year after year, this little girl's anxieties increased as she witnessed her mother's suffering. Grown, with a family of her own, she remained haunted by the cries of her mother.

"No child should ever have to hear that," she said. "I've hated my father most of my life, but I've been praying for heart healing, and I now think of my father differently. I'm forty-five years old, and my heart is finally calm. I have peace.

> "Peace I leave with you; my peace I give you.
> I do not give to you as the world gives.
> Do not let your hearts be troubled and do not be afraid."
>
> — **John 14:27 NIV**

***

I marvel at the continuing stories of miracle moments with God. When we ask, He examines our hearts filled with pain from life's greatest tragedies. Yes, He replaces that pain with peace.

Alex's Story

When Alex's blood pressure rose, as it often did, others in the room could sense the tension. Warned of the dangers of his condition, he considered medications to ease the stress. Then he read about heart healing. Once he realized he could pray at the moment painful memories came to mind, he would respond to a sudden stab in his soul by praying immediately. This is what he told me:

> *"Now I've prayed about millions of memories from the 'old Alex' while driving the Los Angeles freeways*

for work. Whether I thought of an argument I had over fifty years ago, or an embarrassing moment when my boss ridiculed me in front of our sales team, I'd put one hand on my heart and ask God to heal the pain from each bad memory."

Thoughts repeatedly nagging Alex for years were all neutralized by God. His brief freeway prayers brought increased peace, and his chronic high blood pressure lowered dramatically.

***

Abby's Story

For a long time, Abby could not cry. Her carefully guarded heart didn't allow feelings exposed. Frequent flashbacks of hurtful words spoken to her made her feel rejected and wounded, and she'd stuff them back into a secret place. Once she learned how to pray for healing, she opened her heart to Jesus' miraculous healing power. Sometimes it was easy to pray. Other times, she had to make an effort and ask God to help her. With each answered prayer, though, she learned to trust Him more. Her peace steadily increased, and her anxiety disappeared. Now, she writes, "I hear the stories of friends who are struggling with heartache and all I can think is, *Wow, if only they knew how to pray, too.*"

***

These are phenomenal acts of God that cannot be reasoned with our minds. When we hear the stories of others, hope stirs within us. Our hope gathers fragments of faith as we ask Him to help us, too. Even if only one memory is healed at a time, one builds on another and another and another. Eventually, our hearts align with peace more than any of us thought possible. Feelings of joy, often absent from the lives of the hurting, begin to work their way through our hearts, too.

> "May the God of hope fill you with all joy and peace
> as you trust in him,
> so that you may overflow with hope
> by the power of the Holy Spirit."
>
> **— Romans 15:13 NIV**

As we gain this incredible peace, how will we maintain it? There are practical actions we can take, such as avoiding unhealthy relationships, exercising wisdom in our choices of entertainment and access to information, and setting boundaries to protect ourselves from as much emotional trauma as possible.

Eventually, our hearts align with peace more than any of us thought possible. Feelings of joy, often absent from the lives of the hurting, begin to work their way through our hearts, too.

No matter how many measures we take to protect ourselves, tragedies will come. Crises will arise. How will we guard our hearts during the times we cannot control?

In Chapter One, we read King Solomon's words:

> "Above all else, guard your heart,
> for everything you do flows from it."
>
> **— Proverbs 4:23 NIV**

How do we guard our hearts so the things that flow from them inspire good thoughts, actions, and motivations? How do we prevent current trauma from wrecking our peace? Here are God's words straight from the Bible.

> "Do not be anxious about anything, but in every situation, by prayer and petition, with thanksgiving, present your requests to God. And the peace of God, which transcends all understanding, will guard your hearts and your minds in Christ Jesus."
>
> **— Philippians 4:6-7 NIV**

For many years, I misunderstood how to handle crises. Looking closely, I realize God never instructed us to depend upon our bravery and strength to carry us through difficulties. Gentleness and peace come from our ability to—in every situation—trust God, present every concern to Him, and be thankful no matter what the situation or the outcome.

That's the kind of peace no one can understand—even ourselves—because the peace came from God. But, God's peace rests in giving every anxious thought to Him, thanking Him in advance for His answers, and asking Him for our needs in every detail of our lives, including the memories within us that are hurting our hearts and crushing our souls. God wants to provide His strength to us, and He will give us His peace. When God's peace comes, we can't reason it nor explain it. It just is!

> *God's peace rests in giving every anxious thought to Him, thanking Him in advance for His answers, and asking Him for our needs in every detail of our lives, including the memories within us that are hurting our hearts and crushing our souls.*

When a crisis comes, let's turn to Him for help immediately and follow His instructions:

- Pray.
- Ask for the help we need.
- Thank Him in advance for the answers.

These steps guard our hearts, because we depend for help upon the King of Kings and Lord of Lords. He will continue to show us He will rescue us.

> "You will keep in perfect peace those
> whose minds are steadfast,
> because they trust in you."
>
> **— Isaiah 26:3 NIV**

***

During personal times of greatest loss and harshest tragedy, I read and reread an Old Testament story about King Jehoshaphat (ruler of the kingdom of Judah) to remind me of God's strength and power. I often read the story on the edge of my own despair but ended it with renewed confidence that God would take care of me.

People warned King Jehoshaphat a vast army approached to wage war. This terrible army consisted of a combination of three armies united against Judah. Defeat looked certain, but Jehoshaphat gathered his people together to pray to God. Because this was such a critical moment, they fasted from food, focusing on what God would say. While standing in front of everyone gathered in the city of Jerusalem, Jehoshaphat cried out to God and said:

> "We have no power to face this vast army that is attacking us.
> We do not know what to do, but our eyes are on you."
>
> **— 2 Chronicles 20:12 NIV**

Then, one of the leaders in the group announced:

> "This is what the LORD says to you:
> 'Do not be afraid or discouraged because of this vast army.
> For the battle is not yours, but God's.'"
>
> **— 2 Chronicles 20:14-15 NIV**

Then he adds:

> "'You will not have to fight this battle.
> Take up your positions;
>
> stand firm and see the deliverance the LORD will give you,
>
> Judah and Jerusalem. Do not be afraid;
> do not be discouraged.
>
> Go out to face them tomorrow,
> and the LORD will be with you.'"

— 2 Chronicles 20:17 NIV

When Jehoshaphat and the people heard these words, they gratefully fell, worshipping God and praising Him. Early the next morning, they left for the battle, but before they set out, Jehoshaphat gave final instructions:

> "'Listen to me, Judah and people of Jerusalem!
> Have faith in the LORD your God and you will be upheld.'"

— 2 Chronicles 20:20 NIV

The people went before the army and sang:

> "Give thanks to the LORD,
> for his love endures forever."

— 2 Chronicles 20:21 NIV

They asked God for help, praised Him, and thanked Him even before His answers came! How amazingly God responded. Incredibly, as the people of Judah began to sing, God caused the three united armies to begin fighting among themselves and they destroyed each other! When the men of Judah reached the overlook where they knew they'd confront the huge army, they saw dead bodies scattered on the ground. Not one of the enemy soldiers survived.

What a celebration as the people of Judah returned home, rejoicing over the victory brought about because God responded with a mighty miracle. He fought their battle for them because they turned to Him, prayed, and thanked Him even before His remarkable rescue.

The story spread to all the surrounding kingdoms about how the Lord fought the enemies of Judah, leaving all in awe and in respectful fear of Him. This honor and respect for God brought quiet peace to the kingdom of Jehoshaphat.

This is the pattern we talked about earlier. When crises come, we guard our hearts through prayer, asking for help; then, we thank Him in advance for His answers. His response brings us peace and deliverance.

> "LORD, you establish peace for us;
> all that we have accomplished you have done for us."
>
> **— Isaiah 26:12 NIV**

And, the hidden closets in our hearts marked "Brave and Strong?" They will no longer be needed. We'll know when we can tear them down because they'll be empty. As God heals our wounds and cancels their impact on our lives, He provides strength when it's needed, and He will bless us with peace as we pray through each hurtful moment as it occurs.

> "The LORD gives strength to his people;
> the LORD blesses his people with peace."
>
> **— Psalm 29:11 NIV**

***

God speaks to us through His word, and we speak to God through prayer. Page by page, prayer upon prayer, we have learned of His amazing love for us and His readiness to answer our prayers for healing.

Now, He gives us more information about the path to peace.

> "Brothers and sisters,
> think about the things that are good
> and worthy of praise.
>
> Think about the things that are true and honorable
> and right and pure and beautiful and respected.
> Do what you learned and received from me,
> what I told you, and what you saw me do.
>
> And the God who gives peace will be with you."
>
> **— Philippians 4:8-9 NCV**

As our peace increases, we hold on to it by training ourselves to think thoughts honoring God—of things that are right and good and true and pure. With our hearts healed, the influences of stress and trauma no longer alter our patterns of thought toward things like anger, depression, and hopelessness.

* * *

The first words Jesus spoke to His disciples after His resurrection were, "Peace be to you." In the original text, He actually used the word *shalom*, not peace. *Shalom* means so much more than simply peace. It means safety, rest, prosperity, wholeness, welfare, completion, fullness, soundness, and even well-being. So, what did Jesus speak to His disciples? "May you be blessed with safety, with rest, with prosperity, with wholeness, with completion, with fullness, with soundness, with well-being, and with peace."[10]

Above all, Jesus came to this earth to offer forgiveness for our sins, healing for our suffering, a path to peace, and eternal life. As we gain understanding of the Lord's remarkable love for us and His desire for our healing, may His *shalom* increase in all our lives.

Shalom means so much more than simply peace. It means safety, rest, prosperity, wholeness, welfare, completion, fullness, soundness, and even well-being.

LET'S ASK

How has God given me increased peace throughout this book?

_____

_____

_____

_____

_____

_____

_____

What steps do I plan to take to guard my heart and keep peace in my life?

_____

_____

_____

_____

_____

_____

LET'S PRAY

Dear Lord, I have heard many stories throughout this book about Your strength and power and Your extraordinary love for me. Please help me keep all I have learned as permanent lessons for healing and hope. I ask You to remind me You are near and ready to help at any time. I want to spend every day guarding my heart by setting healthy boundaries and choosing to think and speak of things that are good, right, and truthful. When tough times come, I will pray, ask You for help, and thank you for the answers ahead of Your response. My life is in Your hands. Please set it forever toward shalom. Amen.

CHAPTER 10

THE CALL

IMAGINE GOD'S HEART as He observes humanity from His throne. He hears the cries of His people calling His name as they reach out for help. Today's communication networks make us more aware than ever of the tragedies and traumas occurring in our global society, but God's healing touch stretches over all of His creation.

* * *

While my father battled cancer, my husband and I raised four teenagers—with typical adolescent struggles and crises, including one with an incurable condition. Many mornings, heartache chained me to my bed where I would attempt to hide from the world and ignore reality. I often pictured myself alone in a sea of crashing waves, reaching up for God to rescue me before the turmoil destroyed me.

I came to know many people around this world do the same. We hope for help, wondering if it's possible to heal the disturbance in our souls. We become consumed by stress and trauma. We look around us for assistance from caring friends, family members, counselors, pastors, and priests. We look within ourselves to speak affirming words and attempt to redirect our thoughts. With all the heartbreak, everyone seeks an antidote, a remedy, a cure.

While these resources may be very helpful, there is Someone who loves us dearly, who *will* make it all better.

I write these pages hoping to spread the word about God's gift of healing and peace. With your help, and with God's blessing, He will bring peace to many who are in pain.

When He heals you, will you tell others your story?

> "For you have been called to live in freedom,
> my brothers and sisters . . .
> use your freedom to serve one another in love."
>
> **— Galatians 5:13 NLT**

What if more pastors stepped out with specific prayer during services and counseling sessions for hearts to be healed? What if an increasing number of evangelists invited listeners to join them in heart-healing prayer to eradicate pain? What if we told our friends and family members about who God is and what He can do for them? What if, together, we all turned the hearts of the hurting to Someone who will rescue them and give them different tomorrows?

When He heals you, will you tell others your story?

The next time someone dear to us tells us they'll never get over a painful event, we now know what to do.

Let's imagine a world where God sweeps healing through humanity and cancels the efforts of darkness to hold us back from our destiny. Envision a teacher praying for a rejected student, a best friend praying for another by telephone miles away, or a grandparent tenderly praying for a hurting grandchild.

Would prayers for heart healing open doors for missionaries? How could traditional treatments be enhanced through counselors and therapists with specific prayers to our Creator for heart healing? Imagine family members gathering for prayer when a traumatic event occurs.

***

When Dad died, he was well known in the supermarket industry around the state, and especially in our community.

Dad was not a perfect man, but he was well loved. He left a legacy in Texas of hard work, community involvement, compassion, and kindness.

My mom was also kind and compassionate, but by contrast, she preferred her close circle of friends to being in the limelight. When she passed away, a small group of dear friends joined us at the service and supported us with their love.

Yet, her stories of heartbreak inspired me through this book. Somehow I sense her legacy will bless many far beyond the borders of her great state.

> *No matter how many pages of pain are found in our biographies, The Heart Healer is ready to replace each one with peace. With every healed moment and with every step toward a personal relationship with our Creator, He will write the last chapters of our lives to always end in triumph.*

Let's imagine what our legacies will be.

Will we allow God to bring healing to our own hearts, so we will not be held back by our past? Will we reach for a life of significance because He opened the door to our future in answer to our prayers?

No matter how many pages of pain are found in our biographies, The Heart Healer is ready to replace each one with peace. With every healed moment and with every step toward a personal relationship with our Creator, He will write the last chapters of our lives to always end in triumph.

Let's obey the gentle nudge of the Spirit of God and pray for someone else's healing, too—wherever we may be. Together we'll know that our tomorrows will not be like our yesterdays.

"I will give thanks to you, Lord, with all my heart;
I will tell of all your wonderful deeds."

— Psalm 9:1 NIV

"I pray that out of his glorious riches he may strengthen
you with power through his Spirit in your inner being,
so that Christ may dwell in your hearts through faith.
And I pray that you, being rooted and established in love,
may have power, together with all the Lord's holy people,
to grasp how wide and long and high and deep
is the love of Christ, and to know this love that
surpasses knowledge—that you may be filled to the
measure of all the fullness of God."

— Ephesians 3:16-20 NIV

ADDENDUM:

THE ULTIMATE HEARTBREAK

THIS IS THE STORY of the ultimate heartbreak and the most astonishing love.

Jesus, Son of God, came to earth in human form—to give up His life for us—to stand in our place and take on our sins. (Sins are things we do that oppose God's moral rules of conduct.) The willing sacrifice of His life for all of humanity—for all our sins and our healing—required the ultimate gift.

"This is what real love is: It is not our love for God;
it is God's love for us.
He sent his Son to die in our place to take away our sins."

— 1 John 4:10 NCV

Through His gift, Jesus was saying to us, "I'll take responsibility for every sin you'll ever commit. I'll give my life so you may live, free to experience the love of the Father with a future including eternal life."

"Now this is eternal life: that they know you,
the only true God,
and Jesus Christ, whom you have sent."

— John 17:3 NIV

The only requirement for us is to believe in Him and to ask Him to forgive us of our sins. When we choose to believe, we increasingly learn more about His incredible love for us, and for all humanity. Continuing to follow His teachings and live by His examples, our lives become increasingly filled with peace, joy, hope, and much more. Jesus said,

"I am the Living Bread that came down out of heaven.
If anyone eats of this Bread
[believes in Me, accepts Me as Savior],
he will live forever. And the Bread that I will give for the life
of the world is My flesh (body)."

— John 6:51 AMP

During Jesus' ministry on earth, He taught about God's character and His love, using parables and examples of healing, forgiveness, faith, trust, love, and a road map toward peace. When the time came for Him to fulfill the reason He came here, He showed us an example of love so great it is hard to comprehend.

You may have heard Jesus died on a cross for us. It may not have had personal meaning to you, but it was done personally for you. From the night He was taken away from His disciples to be judged, He experienced constant trauma and heartache. What must have made it worse for Him was that Jesus knew what was coming—the humiliation, the ridicule, the torture, and yes, the vicarious trauma of those who loved Him as they watched Him suffer. Much of this suffering occurred before He ever arrived at the place of His crucifixion.

You may have heard Jesus died on a cross for us. It may not have had personal meaning to you, but it was done personally for you.

The placement of each nail, and the entire crucifixion process, was strategically designed to create the slowest and most excruciating death possible. The plan was that victims would hang painfully until their diaphragm spasmed and they suffocated to death. The unbearable pain never ended as every shift of the victim's body brought misery.

Then another agony began for Jesus—a terrible crushing pain deep in the chest as the sac that holds His heart—the pericardium—slowly filled with fluid and began to press on His heart. We know this because when Jesus died, a soldier confirmed His death by piercing His side with a spear.

When he did this, there was suddenly a flow of blood and water (John 19:34). This flow of blood mixed with water is evidence that **Jesus died not the usual crucifixion death by suffocation, but of heart failure (a broken heart)**. This was the ultimate heartbreak. He bore the weight of the sins of all humanity in that one horrific experience. He did it for you and for me.

> "And may you have the power to understand . . . how wide, how long, how high, and how deep his love is."
>
> **— Ephesians 3:18 NLT**

Jesus' story does not end in tragedy but in triumph as He rises to life again on the third day after His death. His fascinating story continues in the final chapters of the books of Matthew, Mark, Luke, and John in the Bible.

Now in heaven, He has the keys to each of our hearts.

He bore the weight of the sins of all humanity in that one horrific experience. He did it for you and for me.

For all of our painful memories behind fortress doors or in secret closets of pain, Jesus waits, ready to unlock the deadbolts. We don't need to make declarations, and we're not required to attend church first. We just ask Him. He shows us how much He cares for us.

God has told us ahead of time; we only need a little faith for Him to respond to our requests.

> "He replied, 'Truly I tell you, if you have faith as small as a mustard seed, you can say to this mountain, "Move from here to there," and it will move. Nothing will be impossible for you.'"
>
> **— Matthew 17:20 NIV**

People seek God through prayer, burdened with heartache and weighed down by experiences. Although their faces and hearts may be guarded, God sees the hope that has pulled them to Him.

Trust makes faith personal. When we trust Him, we're saying we know He can perform miracles, and we believe He will perform them for us.

Stories are told many times in the Bible of how people found Jesus wherever He was and asked for a miracle. They may have only heard about Him and had no idea what it would be like to know Him well. Hope was the reason they came.

They were looking for Someone who would love them and make it all better.

Hope may be why you have read this book.

If so, add to your hope a measure of faith and a dose of trust. With faith, you believe God can perform miraculous deeds. You probably heard of miracles He's performed—not just in biblical times, but in these current days. It's not too big a stretch to have faith God can do astonishing things.

Trust makes faith personal. When we trust Him, we're saying we know He can perform miracles, and we believe He will perform them for us. Jesus said,

> "Don't let your hearts be troubled.
> Trust in God, and trust in me."
>
> **— John 14:1 NCV**

It is often said, "Trust is the perfect antidote for a troubled heart."

Are you ready to trust Him to heal the mangled places in your memories?

You will not be able to think of one distressing event God doesn't already know about. He loves you, and His plans for you are for healing.

Big hurts or small, God—The Heart Healer—heals them all, and every healing is a miracle moment.

ENDNOTES

The following list provides some of the resources used in preparation of the book (other than various Bible verses referenced on the Copyright page). In many cases, the information gathered came from numerous internet resources, which can be obtained through typical browser searches.

About the Cover

- Several sources were used for this information including: Debbie McDaniel, "How to Find Beauty in Brokenness," www.Crosswalk.com, accessed June 22, 2017, http://www.crosswalk.com/faith/women/how-to-find-beauty-in-brokenness.html.

Endnotes

1. "Yes, Broken Hearts are Real. But They're Not What You Think", The Today Show, accessed September 9, 2015, http://www.today.com/health/yes-broken-hearts-are-real-they-re-not-what-you-t42131

2. Dr. Matthew Friedman, Exec. Dir., VA National Center for Post-Traumatic Stress Disorder,"'Soldier's Heart' and 'Shell Shock:' Past Names for PTSD", www.PBS.org, accessed October, 2015, http://www.pbs.org/wgbh/pages/frontline/shows/heart/themes/shellshock.html.

3. Jankowski, Dr. Kay, "PTSD and Physical Health," www.ptsd.va.gov, U.S. Department of Veterans Affairs, PTSD:National Center for PTSD, https://www.ptsd.va.gov/professional/co-occurring/ptsd-physical-health.asp.

4. Cleansing Stream International, under the leadership of Pastor Chris Hayward, has had a strong influence on this work. They may be found at www.cleansingstream.org. Another influential ministry was Restoring the Foundations, at www.restoringthefoundations.org.

5. Judith Orloff, M.D. http://www.drjudithorloff.com/Free-Articles/The-Health-Benefits-of-Tears_copy.htm

6. "Types of Memory," BrainHQ.com, accessed March, 2017, https://www.brainhq.com/brain-resources/memory/types-of-memory

7. Chris Wark, "How to Eliminate Stress," Square One: Healing Cancer Coaching Program Module 6.

8. John J. Parsons, "Nishberei Lev: The Lord is near to the brokenhearted," www.hebrew4christians.com, accessed February, 2017, Tevet 11, 5770, http://www.hebrew4christians.com/Meditations/Brokenhearted/brokenhearted.html.

9. Note: Although our physical hearts are already positioned within our bodies on a vertical axis, the author uses this metaphor to encourage readers to align their innermost beings with The Heart Healer.

10. Jonathan Cahn, "Shalom Alecheim," in *The Book of Mysteries*, Day 137.

ABOUT THE AUTHOR

THERE WERE EARLY INDICATIONS that writing was in Cyndy's future. If her parents had seen her stories being written between the pages of her middle school algebra book during classes, they'd have understood why it was necessary to hire a math tutor later.

Writing took a back seat to "real work," however. Her father was a second-generation grocer who raised his children with the understanding that work was a priority. Cyndy's grocery career began at the age of seven, when she earned money for a princess doll by pushing shopping carts back into their racks.

Pushing shopping carts led to bagging groceries, peeling onions, frying donuts, and ringing up sales. In time, Cyndy managed one of the family supermarkets and served as the Human Resource Director for up to 1,000 employees.

The lessons learned about productivity, training, and work ethics carried on for years as she applied these experiences in her adult life. Owning supermarkets overlapped with owning real estate, which evolved into owning a residential real estate investment company.

These were all fantastic experiences, but along the way, sickness, disease, divorce, death, financial loss and more wove their way into the road map of Cyndy's life. She discovered that her own pain led to her passion for helping others who were hurting, too. Eventually, she was able to devote increasing amounts of time to learning about God's extraordinary love for all.

This commitment resulted in a move from Texas to California for Cyndy and her husband. There they have had remarkable experiences learning more about The Heart Healer and the tender way He restores the hearts of the hurting and gives hope to the hopeless.

The Texan Bartellis reside in the Los Angeles area where they spend as much time as possible with their four children and six grandchildren.

Prayer in Seven Simple Steps

—1—

Ask God to reveal the memory He plans to heal.

—2—

Place your hand over your heart.

—3—

Invite the Lord into your heart.

—4—

Ask Him to heal the pain connected to the memory (memories).

—5—

Ask Him to heal any related illness in your mind or body and restore you to good health.

—6—

Thank God for your healing.

—7—

Breathe again!

Learn more at:
CYNDYBARTELLI.COM

Cut out and use this bookmark to as a resource and reminder as you continue to pray and study God's word.

69025446R00112

Made in the USA
Lexington, KY
24 October 2017